STARLING

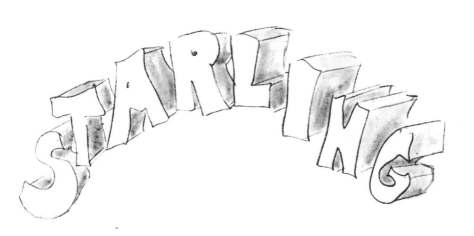

STARLING

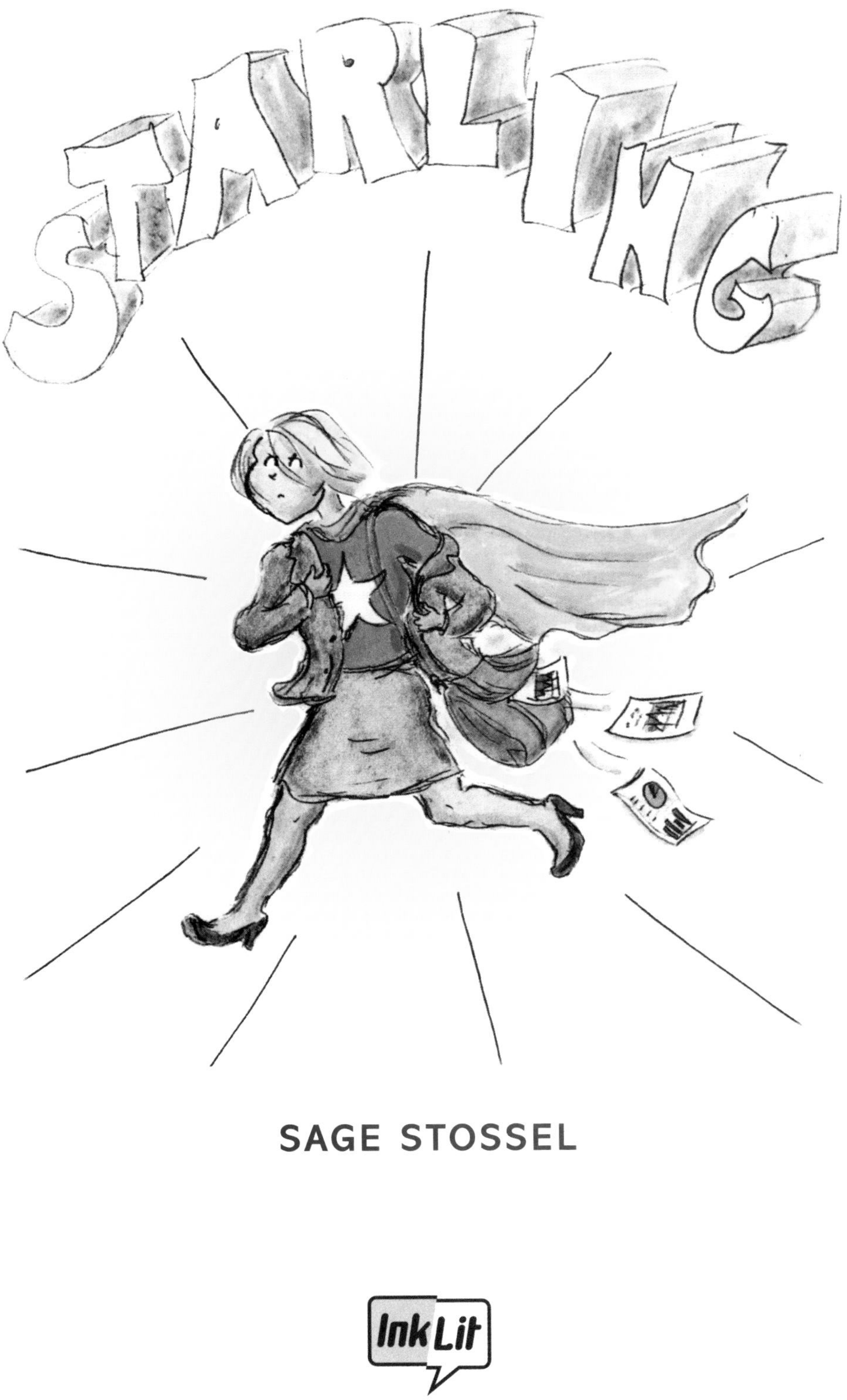

SAGE STOSSEL

InkLit

THE BERKLEY PUBLISHING GROUP
Published by the Penguin Group
Penguin Group (USA) LLC
375 Hudson Street, New York, New York 10014

USA • Canada • UK • Ireland • Australia • New Zealand • India • South Africa • China

penguin.com

A Penguin Random House Company

This book is an original publication of The Berkley Publishing Group.

Library of Congress Cataloging-in-Publication Data

Stossel, Sage, 1971–
Starling / by Sage Stossel. — InkLit trade paperback edition.
pages cm
ISBN 978-0-425-26631-1 (pbk.)
1. Graphic novels. I. Title.
PN6727.S748S73 2013
741.5'973—dc23
2013027141

PUBLISHING HISTORY
InkLit trade paperback edition / December 2013

PRINTED IN THE UNITED STATES OF AMERICA

10 9 8 7 6 5 4 3 2 1

Cover art by Sage Stossel.
Cover design by Sarah Oberrender.

MY THERAPY SESSION WAS GOING AROUND IN ITS USUAL CIRCLES.

...but it's not like you procrastinate and sabotage yourself when it comes to your professional work.

That's because I choose my work.

This other stuff just gets dumped on me at random, inconvenient times.

It's not like I'm even getting paid to -

BZZZ

AS IF TO ILLUSTRATE MY POINT, MY ALARM STARTED BUZZING.

Crud! You see what I mean?

BZZZZ

BUT AS SUMMONSES GO, THIS ONE ACTUALLY WASN'T THAT BAD.

DR. MORRIS, AFTER ALL, WAS ONE OF TWO PEOPLE WHO KNEW THE IMPORTANT FACTS ABOUT ME.

...WHICH FOR ONCE MEANT THAT I WOULDN'T HAVE TO GO SLINKING OFF TO A PUBLIC RESTROOM SOMEWHERE.

I'll leave you to get changed.

AS USUAL, THOUGH, I DILLYDALLIED WAY TOO LONG.

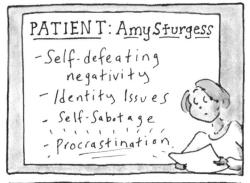

PATIENT: Amy Sturgess
- Self-defeating negativity
- Identity Issues
- Self-Sabotage
- Procrastination

You done in there?

Crud.

...AND THINGS BECAME A MAD SCRAMBLE AFTER ALL.

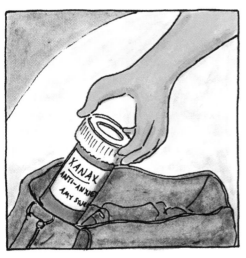

FINALLY I WAS ON MY WAY...

?!

I WOULD MUCH RATHER HAVE BEEN AT HOME WATCHING TV.

In the criminal Justice system...

BUT THIS WAS A PRETTY ROUTINE CALL. BY NOW I COULD PRACTICALLY DO THIS STUFF IN MY SLEEP.

ALERT:
Bank robbery in progress, 9th & 4th St.

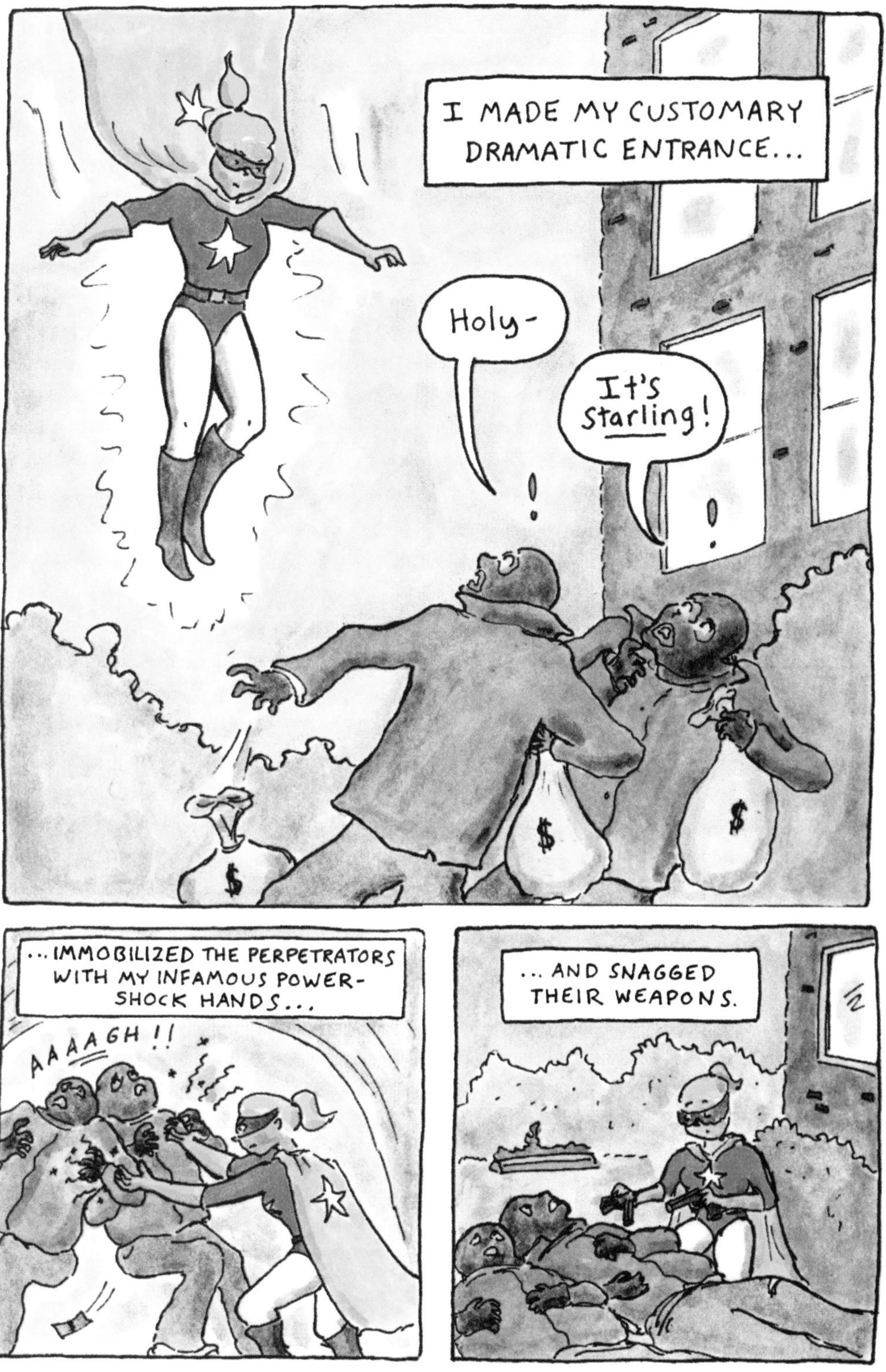
I MADE MY CUSTOMARY DRAMATIC ENTRANCE...
Holy-
It's Starling!
...IMMOBILIZED THE PERPETRATORS WITH MY INFAMOUS POWER-SHOCK HANDS...
AAAAGH!!
...AND SNAGGED THEIR WEAPONS.

THEN I WENT INTO THE BANK TO CHECK THINGS OUT.

FIRST UNITED BANK

IT WAS ONE OF THOSE FINANCIAL DISTRICT "WEALTH-MANAGEMENT" INSTITUTIONS THAT CATERS TO RICH TRADERS AND THEIR FAMILIES.

THE FAT-CAT PATRONS WERE A LITTLE FREAKED-OUT, BUT BASICALLY FINE.

PROBABLY BETTER THAN FINE: THEY'D BE THE LIFE OF THE PARTY FOR YEARS TO COME.

I WENT BACK OUTSIDE TO DEAL WITH MY PERPETRATORS.

LIKE ME, THESE GUYS HAD TO WEAR MASKS TO DO THEIR DIRTY WORK.

...AND THEY LOOKED ABOUT AS MANGY AND WRECKED AS I'D BEEN FEELING LATELY.

THEIR GUNS DIDN'T EVEN HAVE AMMO.

I SEARCHED THEIR POCKETS FOR OTHER WEAPONS...

...BUT ALL I FOUND WAS A BUNCH OF RANDOM JUNK.

FORECLOSURE NOTICE

Eviction proceedings

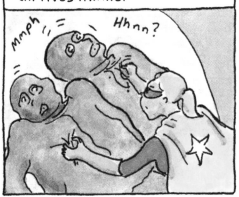

AS A POLICE SIREN STARTED UP IN THE DISTANCE, I SHOOK MY CAPTIVES AWAKE.

Mmph

Hhnn?

THE PLAN WAS TO LEAVE THEM TIED UP FOR THE POLICE WITH A NOTE.

All yours
xoxo
—Starling

LATELY, THOUGH, STICKING TO PLANS HADN'T BEEN MY STRONG SUIT.

Go!

I said Go!

?!

OFF THEY SCRAMBLED, THOUGH NOT BEFORE I GRABBED THE MANGIER ONE AND SHOVED A WAD OF BILLS INTO HIS HAND.

EXEMPLARY SUPERHERO BEHAVIOR?

NOT REALLY.

BUT WHAT CAN I SAY?

Bzzz
Bzzz
Bzzz

I NEVER CLAIMED THAT AS SUPERHEROES GO, I DON'T KIND OF SUCK.

Yeah, this is Dr. Morris. I just wanted to let you know your socks are under my desk.

OF COURSE, EVEN APART FROM MY LACKLUSTER SUPERHEROING, I'M OFTEN ACCUSED OF HAVING A BAD ATTITUDE.

... BUT IN FACT I THINK I'M PRETTY WELL-ADJUSTED FOR SOMEONE RAISED IN A HOUSE WITH 36 CATS.

MOM WAS PRETTY AFFECTIONATE WITH THE CATS.

... BUT NOT SO MUCH WITH THE REST OF US.

The Sturgess Family

WHATEVER. EVERYONE KNOWS ANIMAL HOARDERS ARE WEIRD. I TRY NOT TO TAKE IT PERSONALLY.

SCHOOL WAS PRETTY UNPLEASANT, THOUGH.

THE KIDS WHO SAID I SMELLED LIKE CAT PEE WEREN'T WRONG.

I GOT PRETTY GOOD AT PRETENDING NOT TO HEAR.

No—you sit next to her!

Eww! No way!!

...AND PRETTY GOOD AT AMUSING MYSELF.

AT ADOLESCENCE, WEIRD THINGS STARTED HAPPENING...

Put tools AWAY when shop class is over!!

Listen up, girls— we're going to do sprints.

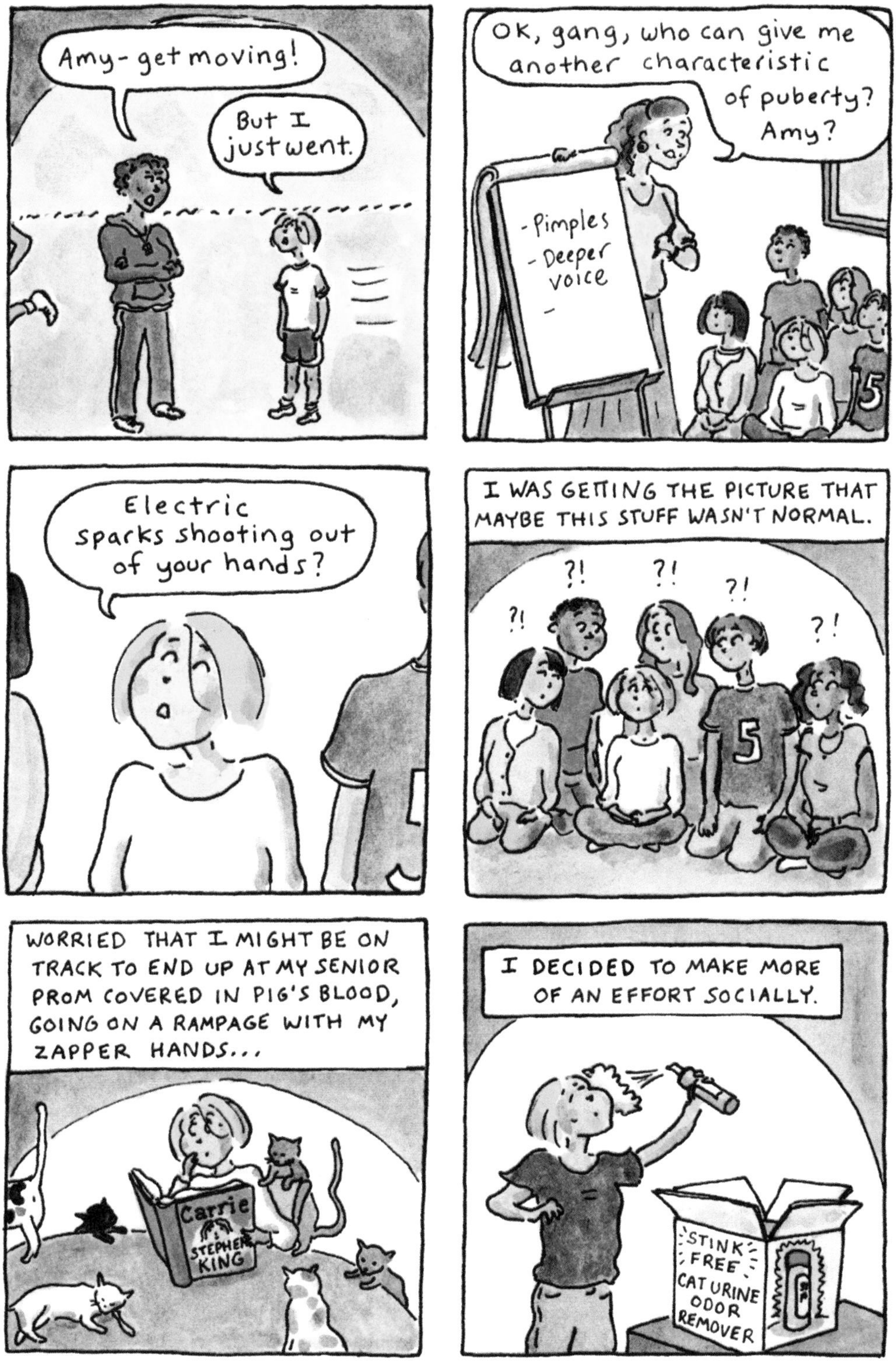
Amy- get moving!
But I just went.
Ok, gang, who can give me another characteristic of puberty? Amy?
- Pimples
- Deeper voice
-
Electric sparks shooting out of your hands?
I WAS GETTING THE PICTURE THAT MAYBE THIS STUFF WASN'T NORMAL.
?!
?!
?!
?!
?!
WORRIED THAT I MIGHT BE ON TRACK TO END UP AT MY SENIOR PROM COVERED IN PIG'S BLOOD, GOING ON A RAMPAGE WITH MY ZAPPER HANDS...
Carrie
STEPHEN KING
I DECIDED TO MAKE MORE OF AN EFFORT SOCIALLY.
STINK FREE
CAT URINE ODOR REMOVER

Is this seat taken?

Nope.

I HARDLY BECAME MS. POPULARITY...

BUT MY CLASSMATES DID DEVELOP A BASIC TOLERANCE FOR MY ECCENTRICITIES.

Did you just reheat that potato with your hand?

Cool.

ONE NIGHT, IN THE SPRING OF MY 10TH-GRADE YEAR, THE SCHOOL MADE US ALL STAY LATE TO WATCH THE DRAMA CLUB'S PRODUCTION OF TWELFTH NIGHT.

I DIDN'T FEEL LIKE GETTING DROPPED OFF AT MY CAT-INFESTED HOUSE IN FRONT OF MY CLASSMATES AFTERWARDS, SO I DITCHED THE BUS.

My Mom's picking me up.

THE MAN WHO ACCOSTED ME ON CLARK AVENUE SEEMED LIKE A REGULAR GUY— AT LEAST AT FIRST.

Sorry to bother you—do you know what time it is?

8:30

Thanks...can I ask a favor?

...I have this sheet cake in my van that I have to bring up to my friend's apartment.

THE SITUATION WAS SEEMING SKETCHIER AND SKETCHIER.

BUT FOR THE FIRST TIME EVER, I WAS FACING A PROBLEM I KNEW EXACTLY HOW TO HANDLE.

...AND THE PROBLEM HAD NO CLUE WHAT WAS COMING...

MY HANDS WERE TINGLING AND SPARKING.

I COULD FEEL THE CHARGE SURGING OUT FROM MY FINGERS.

IT WAS A GOOD QUESTION. I HAD ABSOLUTELY NO IDEA.

BUT HE FAINTED BEFORE I COULD EVEN TRY TO ANSWER.

I DRAGGED HIM TO THE POLICE STATION.

...WHERE I FOISTED HIM OFF ON THE FIRST COP I COULD FIND.

POLICE

I'D ASSUMED I COULD JUST DROP HIM OFF AND GO HOME. BUT THEY MADE ME GO OVER AND OVER WHAT HAPPENED.

He wanted me to go in his van.

MEANWHILE, THE GUY HAD APPARENTLY COME TO AND WAS IN ANOTHER ROOM, TELLING A DIFFERENT STORY.

He says you attacked him out of nowhere with bolts of electricity.

Do you have a stun gun?

No.

THEY DIDN'T FIND ME IN THE SYSTEM, BUT THEY DID FIND MY MOM, WHO WAS ON RECORD FOR POSSESSION OF 36 UNLICENSED CATS.

I WAS STARTING TO WORRY IT WAS *ME* WHO WAS GOING TO WIND UP IN TROUBLE.

BUT ABRUPTLY THEY SAID I COULD GO.

APPARENTLY THEY'D CHECKED THE GUY'S VAN AND FOUND EVIDENCE LINKING HIM TO MISSING KIDS IN 3 OTHER STATES.

I WAS RELIEVED TO LEARN THE KIDS WERE FOUND SAFE IN THE GUY'S GARAGE.

WTPX

BUT FOR DAYS AFTERWARDS I COULD HARDLY SLEEP.

THE STORY GOT WRITTEN UP IN THE PAPER WITH ME AS THE HEROINE.

10TH GRADER FOILS SERIAL ATTACKER

THEY DIDN'T GIVE ME FULL CREDIT, THOUGH.

HERALD-JOURNAL

Police speculate that Mr. Buford may have stumbled onto a downed power line and suffered a mild heart attack "Giv..

AT SCHOOL, THE EPISODE EARNED ME A FLURRY OF EMBARRASS-ING ATTENTION.

Yo, Sturgess— bust any heads lately?

...WHILE AT HOME, MY PARENTS WERE AS OBLIVIOUS AS EVER.

Amy, what did you do with the cat brush?

10TH GRADER FOILS SERIAL ATTACKER

BUT MY LITTLE BROTHER, NOAH, STARTED FOLLOW-ING ME AROUND LIKE A GROUPIE.

Show me again how you punched him in the face!

THAT PART I DIDN'T MIND SO MUCH.

...so then I grabbed him...

TWO WEEKS LATER, A LETTER ARRIVED.

IT WAS AN INVITATION TO MEET WITH THE LOCAL BRANCH OF SOMETHING CALLED THE VIGILANTE JUSTICE ASSOCIATION.

Dear Ms. Sturgess, Having read in the Herald-Journal of your courageous actions on the night of April 23, we would like to set up a meeting with you. Please call us at (555) 347-1279.
Sincerely,

IT WAS SO RARE THAT I EVER GOT INVITED ANYWHERE THAT I COULDN'T RESIST.

Yes, this is Amy Sturgess...

THE ADDRESS WAS A DOWN-TOWN OFFICE BUILDING.

17
18 WALSH, Inc
19
20 M. D'ORSI ESQ
21
22 V.J.A
24 MORSE ADVISORS
35
36 PMX SYSTEMS

A MAN INTRODUCING HIMSELF AS ROY VANCE USHERED ME INTO HIS OFFICE.

THE NEWSPAPER STORY WAS ON HIS DESK.

That's quite a run-in you had the other night.

So was the perpetrator really disabled by a downed power line, like the police are saying?

No.

You took him out yourself?

Yes.

And electricity was involved?

From my hands, yes.

Do you have any other unusual physical abilities?

Strength.

Anything else?

Speed.

What about flight?

No.

What is this? Twenty Questions?

It doesn't exactly require some big research project to figure out I'm a freak show.

Not a freak show, Amy. I think you have some genetic mutations that give you unusual abilities.

"I'm just trying to get a handle on what yours are. It's what we specialize in here."

"Do you mind if my staff puts you through a few tests?"

UNLIKE SCHOOL, WHERE I WAS INCESSANTLY FALLING SHORT ON TESTS I HADN'T PREPARED FOR, THESE TESTS WERE GRATIFYINGLY EASY.

...AT LEAST FOR THE MOST PART.
"OK, now what letters am I holding up on the other side of the wall?"

EV5B
TXLP
RVW2

MT
XLP
RTN
256
ZL

X-RAY VISION
YES ☐
NO ☒

I WAS ACTUALLY DISAPPOINTED WHEN THE TESTS WERE OVER.
"Have a seat."

"Your range of abilities is limited."

"X-ray vision, invisibility, shape-shifting... None of those things are in your repertoire."

"But your strength and speed — they're off the charts."

And the voltage in your hands is extraordinary.

Is it static electricity from all the cats in my house?

?

No, it's clear that you're generating the electricity yourself.

...most likely as a result of having been exposed to something mutagenic as a young child—like radiation or some kind of toxic substance.

I THOUGHT OF THE PICTURE IN THE FRONT HALL OF MOM, PREGNANT WITH ME AT HER OLD JOB CLEANING TEST TUBES AT THE MILITARY LAB ON RT. 97.

But there's something else...

It would be highly unusual for your cluster of abilities to present without flight as a corollary.

?

He means we think you can fly.

But I can't fly. It's not like I would be hiding it from you if I could.

See...I'm trying right now, and I don't see anything happening, do you?

It doesn't work that way.

It's an ability that requires a situation of absolute necessity to kick in.

You mean it stays dormant unless I fall out a window or something?

Exactly.

AND SO TEN MINUTES LATER I FOUND MYSELF QUAKING ON THE RAILING OF THE 22ND-FLOOR BALCONY WHILE TWO PEOPLE I'D BARELY JUST MET URGED ME TO JUMP.

Is flight really worth possibly smashing my head open for?

We wouldn't know — neither of us can fly.

Great-easy to make your guests dive off the balcony...

BUT WHEN I THOUGHT OF THE GEOMETRY TEST I HADN'T STUDIED FOR...

...AND THE ANNOYING CLIQUES AT SCHOOL...

...AND THE MANGY CATS LEAVING KITTY LITTER ALL OVER MY PILLOW...

...IT SEEMED LIKE MAYBE NOT SUCH A TERRIBLE RISK AFTER ALL.

OVER THE RAIL I WENT.

...AND PROCEEDED TO PLUMMET HELPLESSLY.

THE DESCENT WAS ALL
AT ONCE BREAK-
NECK FAST...

...AND SLOW-MOTION
DISASTER SLOW.

AN ELDERLY WOMAN
STEPPED OUT THE
DOOR OF THE BUILD-
ING AND LOOKED UP.

OUR EYES MET AND WE BOTH
SHRIEKED AS I BRACED FOR IMPACT.

BUT THEN...

SUDDENLY THE LADY
WAS NOWHERE IN SIGHT
AND I WAS GLIDING...

...ANGLING UPWARDS...

... LOOKING DOWN ON PEOPLE ...

... AND DIRECTLY INTO PEOPLE'S OFFICE WINDOWS.

... AND CARS ...

I COULD SWOOP AND CHANGE DIRECTION AT WILL, JUST BY LEANING ONE WAY OR THE OTHER.

Oh my God—you guys have to come see this !!!

Crud.

I HURRIED BACK TO THE V.J.A. BALCONY BEFORE I COULD TURN INTO A PUBLIC SPECTACLE.

Look at you!

We thought you could do it!

And what if I couldn't? Were you really going to just scrape me off the sidewalk?

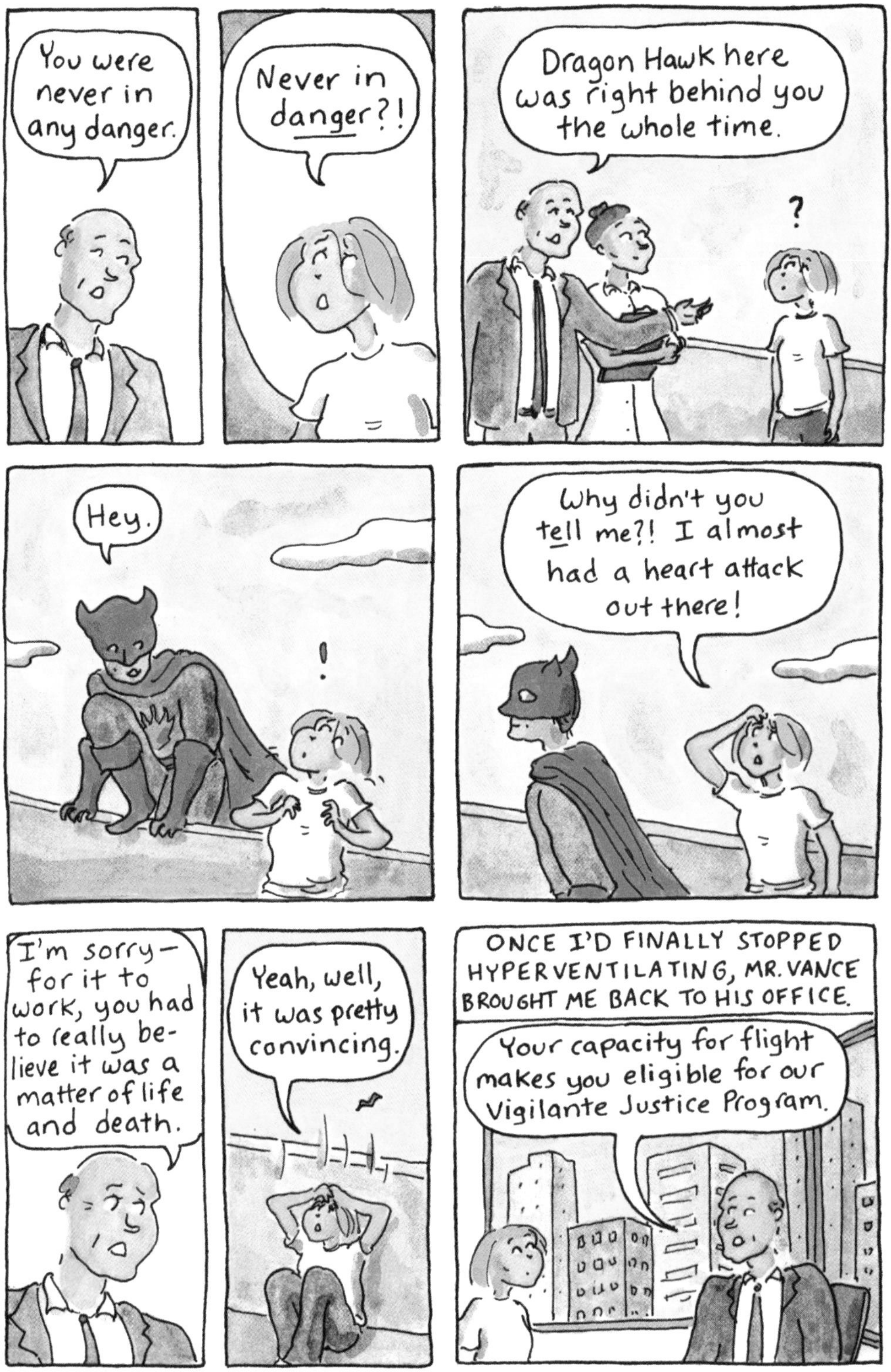
You were never in any danger.
Never in danger?!
Dragon Hawk here was right behind you the whole time.
?
Hey.
!
Why didn't you tell me?! I almost had a heart attack out there!
I'm sorry— for it to work, you had to really believe it was a matter of life and death.
Yeah, well, it was pretty convincing.
ONCE I'D FINALLY STOPPED HYPERVENTILATING, MR. VANCE BROUGHT ME BACK TO HIS OFFICE.
Your capacity for flight makes you eligible for our Vigilante Justice Program.

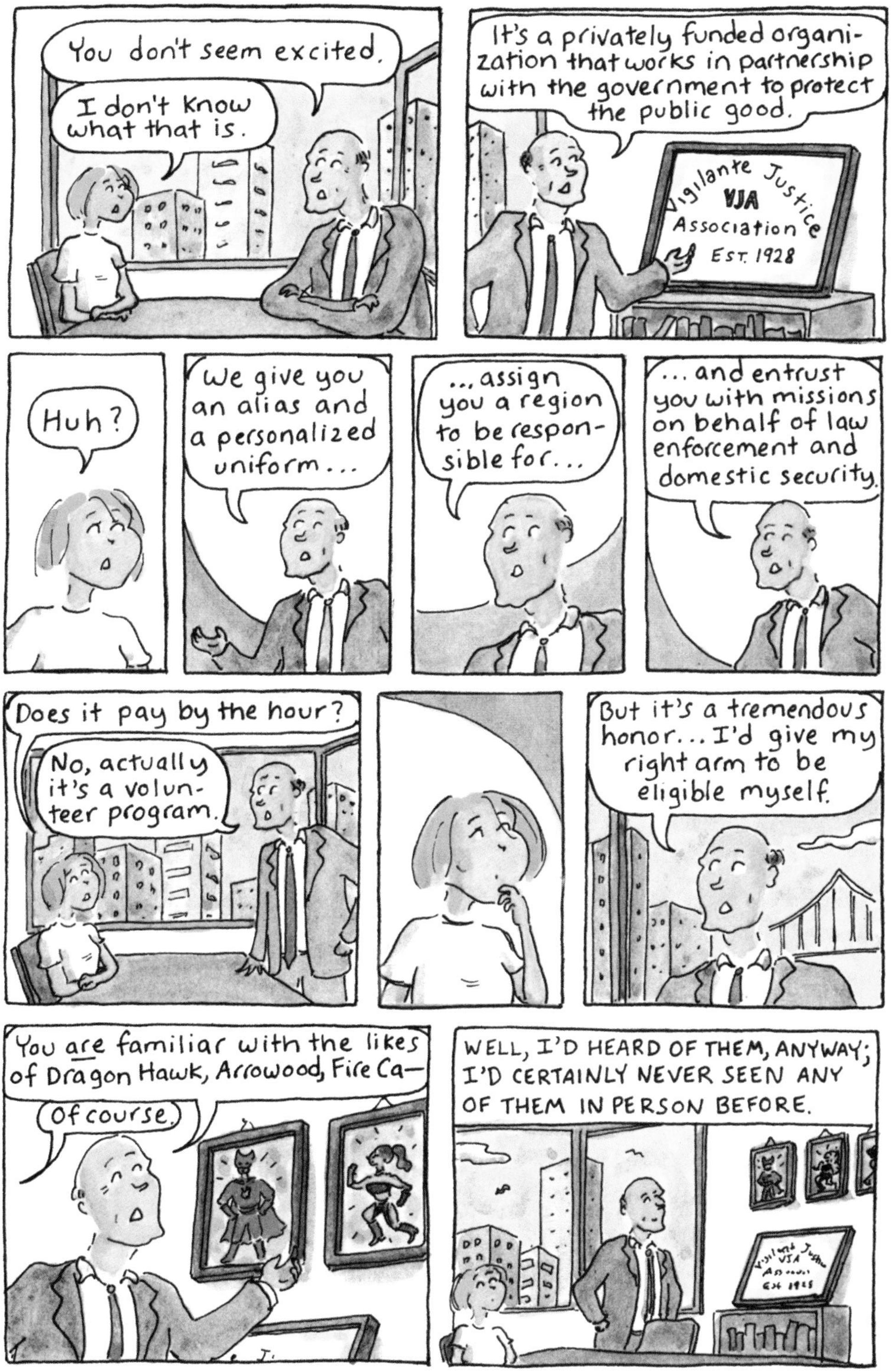
You don't seem excited.
I don't know what that is.
It's a privately funded organization that works in partnership with the government to protect the public good.
Vigilante Justice VJA Association Est. 1928
Huh?
We give you an alias and a personalized uniform...
...assign you a region to be responsible for...
...and entrust you with missions on behalf of law enforcement and domestic security.
Does it pay by the hour?
No, actually it's a volunteer program.
But it's a tremendous honor... I'd give my right arm to be eligible myself.
You are familiar with the likes of Dragon Hawk, Arrowood, Fire Ca—
Of course.
WELL, I'D HEARD OF THEM, ANYWAY; I'D CERTAINLY NEVER SEEN ANY OF THEM IN PERSON BEFORE.

Hey, sorry to interrupt.

I just wanted to let you know the Canadian pirate's been turned over to Homeland Security.

Ok, thanks.

Wouldn't you like to join their ranks?

AS ARRANGEMENTS GO, IT SOUNDED PRETTY CRAPPY...LIKE SIGNING UP FOR THE NATIONAL GUARD FOR NO PAY OR RECOGNITION.

BUT I WAS A SUCKER FOR THE CHANCE TO FEEL LIKE SOMETHING SPECIAL FOR ONCE.

Vigilante Jus

OF COURSE, I SAID YES.

Welcome aboard.

AND SO, AFTER A BIT OF TRIAL AND ERROR ON THE COSTUME FRONT...

No.

No.

Who's your costume designer? A thirteen-year-old boy?

Actually, yes.

This is my son, Roy Jr.

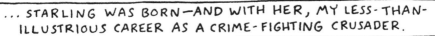

... STARLING WAS BORN—AND WITH HER, MY LESS-THAN-ILLUSTRIOUS CAREER AS A CRIME-FIGHTING CRUSADER.

You do realize that outfit is totally 1970s?...

TEN YEARS LATER, I'D WORKED HARD TO PUT MY AWKWARD CHILDHOOD BEHIND ME.

I'D SQUEAKED INTO A REPUTABLE COLLEGE DESPITE LACKLUSTER GRADES.

...AND FOLLOWING THE LEAD OF MY COOL, WORLDLY ROOMMATE, I'D CHOSEN MARKETING AS MY MAJOR.

FOR ONCE I'D APPLIED MYSELF AND HAD ACTUALLY EXCELLED.

NOW, SEVERAL YEARS OUT OF SCHOOL, AN INTERNSHIP AT A GOOD FIRM HAD TURNED INTO A REAL JOB.

...AND I WAS WORKING HARD TO PROVE MYSELF.

BUT THAT ANNOYING EMERGENCY BUZZER WAS BECOMING THE BANE OF MY EXISTENCE.

IT WOULD GO OFF AT ANY HOUR OF THE DAY OR NIGHT...

...AT THE WORST POSSIBLE TIMES.

...FORCING ME TO SCRAMBLE INTO MY STRETCHY, LITTLE, HARD-TO-PUT-ON OUTFIT WITH NO TIME TO SPARE.

THEN, OF COURSE, I'D HAVE TO GO KNOCK HEADS TOGETHER, WHETHER I FELT UP TO IT OR NOT.

ON TOP OF THAT, I HAD TO MAKE EXCUSES FOR MYSELF.

...WHICH MADE IT MORE THAN A LITTLE DIFFICULT TO MAINTAIN MUCH OF A SOCIAL LIFE TO SPEAK OF.

YEARS EARLIER, I'D LEARNED THE HARD WAY THAT JUST RUNNING OUT OF A ROOM WITH NO EXPLANATION DOESN'T GO OVER TOO WELL.

Amy Sturgess—where do you think you're going?!

$x^2 + y^2 - 2x$
$D = (-m)^2$
$\pi 4^2$
$m^2 - 8m^2$

SO I'D TAKEN TO TELLING PEOPLE I HAD IRRITABLE BOWEL SYNDROME

"...severe, unpredictable intestinal distress..."

IRRITABLE BOWEL SYNDROME
IBS

AT LEAST THAT WAY IF I SUDDENLY SPRINTED TO THE NEAREST BATHROOM TO CHANGE, PEOPLE DIDN'T ASK TOO MANY QUESTIONS.

BUT IT WAS DEPRESSING TO RETURN FROM SOME HARROWING, EXHAUSTING MISSION ONLY TO HAVE EVERYONE ASSUME I'D BEEN SITTING ON THE TOILET FOR AN HOUR.

Need a Pepto?

SOMETIMES I WONDERED WHAT INTESTINAL AGONIES THEY THOUGHT I'D BEEN GOING THROUGH IN THOSE BATHROOM STALLS.

MY THERAPIST CLAIMED IT WAS THE PRESSURES OF MY DOUBLE LIFE THAT KEPT ME SO FOCUSED AT WORK.

BUT REALLY IT WAS A MATTER OF MY WORKING THREE TIMES AS HARD AS ANYONE JUST TO NOT GET LEFT IN THE DUST.

9:00 PM

ONE AFTERNOON, I RETURNED FROM YET ANOTHER MID-WORKDAY EMERGENCY CALL TO FIND A NOTE ON MY DESK.

Dan came by—
Wants to know if U can take on the Health Mark Account ???

I WENT TO INVESTIGATE.

Hey, Dan. You were looking for me?

Yeah—no worries.

I found Jason. He says he can take this one on.

AFTER WORK THAT EVENING, MY COLLEAGUE DINA WAS INDIGNANT ON MY BEHALF.

That's such B.S. Jason doesn't know the first thing about the health care market.

Yeah, well— I wasn't around.

A RISING STAR AT THE COMPANY, DINA HAD STARTED AT MARKET WORKS SIX MONTHS BEFORE ME. HAPPILY FOR ME, SHE'D APPOINTED HERSELF MY UNOFFICIAL MENTOR AND GUIDE.

Dan could have waited till you got back.

Yeah, but you know Jason— he was probably lying in wait to jump out and steal that account the second I wasn't available.

What an operator.

You know he'll probably try to pick your brain and make it look like it's all him.

He's done it before.

I know.

It sucks that the irritable bowel thing puts you out of commission so much.

Have you ever thought of trying one of those colonic cleanses? They're supposed to be really helpful for people with unpredictable explosive diarrhea.

AS USUAL, MY PROSPECTS FOR ANY KIND OF DATING LIFE WERE NOT LOOKING GOOD.

Hey, that guy was cute!

Yeah, well—I think we lost him at "explosive diarrhea."

I don't see why you don't sign up for Match.com. I would have done it if I hadn't met Rob.

You would have done what if you hadn't met me?

LUCKILY FOR BOSSY DINA, SHE'D MANAGED TO FIND THE WORLD'S MOST ACCOMMODATING BOYFRIEND.

THEY WERE ENGAGED NOW— GETTING MARRIED IN JUST A FEW WEEKS.

You about ready to hit the road?

Sure—I'm ready if you are.

AT HOME THAT NIGHT, I COULDN'T RESIST A LITTLE ONLINE BROWSING.

LOOKING FOR:

Nice, handsome, impervious to electricity up to 750 volts.

SEARCH

You have:

0 results

THE CLOSEST I'D EVER COME TO HAVING A BOYFRIEND WAS MY JUNIOR YEAR IN COLLEGE.

DRISCOLL U YEARBOOK

RUSSELL WAS MY ASSIGNED IN-CLASS STUDY PARTNER FOR FRENCH II.

Je suis, tu es, nous sommes...

WHEN THE INSTRUCTOR SAID WE HAD TO COME UP WITH A SKIT TO PRESENT TO THE CLASS, WE STARTED MEETING UP OUTSIDE OF CLASS, TOO.

No— I should hold the guillotine, because you need a free hand to throw Marie Antoinette's head.

EVEN AFTER THE CLASS WAS OVER, WE STILL MET UP FOR LUNCH SOMETIMES DURING THE SPRING SEMESTER.

Ça va?

Oui.

AND WHEN JUNIOR FORMAL TIME ROLLED AROUND, WE DECIDED TO GO TOGETHER.

SPRING FORMAL Friday 8PM–1 AM

Andy Margulies's brother is DJing.

Cool.

THE DANCE WAS FUN.

You look mahvelous.

You, too, dahlink.

AFTERWARDS, WE CLIMBED UP OBSERVATORY HILL TO CHECK OUT THE VIEW.

Is that Mars?

I think that's the light on the Hillsboro Sunoco station.

A MISTY RAIN STARTED UP.

Are you cold?

A little.

HE GAVE ME HIS JACKET.

Amy, I—

ZAP

Crud.

I'D ACCIDENTALLY FRIED HIM WITH A BURST OF ELECTRICITY FROM MY HANDS.

AS HE RECOVERED AT THE HOSPITAL, I FRETTED OVER WHAT TO TELL HIM.

BUT AS IT TURNED OUT, I DIDN'T NEED TO WORRY.

I'm sorry—we should never have gone up there in a storm.

I didn't even hear the thunder.

Yeah—me neither...

I DECIDED TO BREAK THINGS OFF, FEARING I MIGHT PERMANENTLY INJURE HIM NEXT TIME.

BEING A WIMP, I HANDLED IT BY SIMPLY AVOIDING HIM.

If that's Russell, I'm not here.

BRRRINNG

DRISCOLL U

FOR A WHILE HE GAVE ME HURT LOOKS ACROSS THE DINING HALL.

BUT EVENTUALLY I STARTED NOTICING HIM AROUND WITH A SOPHOMORE NAMED CLAIRE.

SHE SEEMED SWEET AND PULLED TOGETHER.

CLEARLY HIS TASTE HAD IMPROVED.

I HOPED THAT KNOWING HE'D MOVED ON WOULD ONCE AND FOR ALL GET ME TO STOP THINKING ABOUT HIM.

Hey, Russell — Long time no talk... Any chance you feel like catching up one of these days?

BUT LAMELY, I'D CONTINUED TO KEEP TABS ON HIM—FOLLOWING HIS PROGRESS THROUGH LAW SCHOOL AND NOW AS A FIRST-YEAR ASSOCIATE IN TOWN.

RUSSELL HICKS graduated with honors from Driscoll University then obtained his JD from the University of

I EVEN HAD A STALKERISH **HABIT** OF FLYING **PAST** HIS APARTMENT ON MY WAY BACK FROM EMERGENCY CALLS.

HE SEEMED TO BE DOING PRETTY WELL.

CLAIRE, TOO.

I HAD TO ADMIT, MY OWN LIFE PALED A BIT IN COMPARISON.

Our Saved by the Bell marathon continues in just a moment.

AT WORK THE NEXT DAY, JASON WAS HIS USUAL CONNIVING SELF.

Hey, Amy—Do you have any focus group data you can lend me on the patient-care amenities market?

IT WAS MY AREA OF EXPERTISE, WHICH WAS PRECISELY WHY THE HEALTHMARK ACCOUNT WAS SUPPOSED TO HAVE BEEN ASSIGNED TO ME.

NO WAY WAS I DOING HIS WORK FOR HIM LIKE USUAL.

Sorry— my data's kind of old. It probably wouldn't be relevant.

That's ok. Mind if I just take a peek anyway?

You know, I'm actually not even sure where those files are right now.

HEALTH CARE

You can't find them?

You know how it is when you've been juggling so many accounts.

LESS THAN HALF AN HOUR LATER, I STUMBLED ONTO JASON HAVING A WORD WITH DAN OUTSIDE THE MEN'S ROOM.

I just think she's stressed out.

She says she can't even manage to keep her working data up-to-date, and she has so many accounts she can't keep track of them all.

"I think—" "Just speaking as her friend, and totally in confidence, I know Amy would really appreciate a less intense workload."

HOLY CRAP. I WAS SO FURIOUS, MY HANDS WERE SPARKING.

WHEN I'D SOMEWHAT COLLECTED MYSELF, I MARCHED INTO DAN'S OFFICE.

"Can I talk to you for a minute?"

"Sure—I was actually going to come find you."

"I know what Jason told you."

"About your workload?"

"Yes."

"You're finding things a little too much?"

"No! He makes stuff up! I don't know what his problem is."

POOR DAN HAD A NEWBORN AT HOME AND HAD HARDLY SLEPT IN A MONTH AND A HALF.

"〈Sigh〉"

"Amy, I have to be honest with you..."

UH-OH. THIS WASN'T SOUNDING LIKE IT WAS ABOUT TO GO THE WAY I'D HOPED.

"I know Jason exaggerates sometimes, and he's not exactly a fount of innovative ideas."

"But he's here."

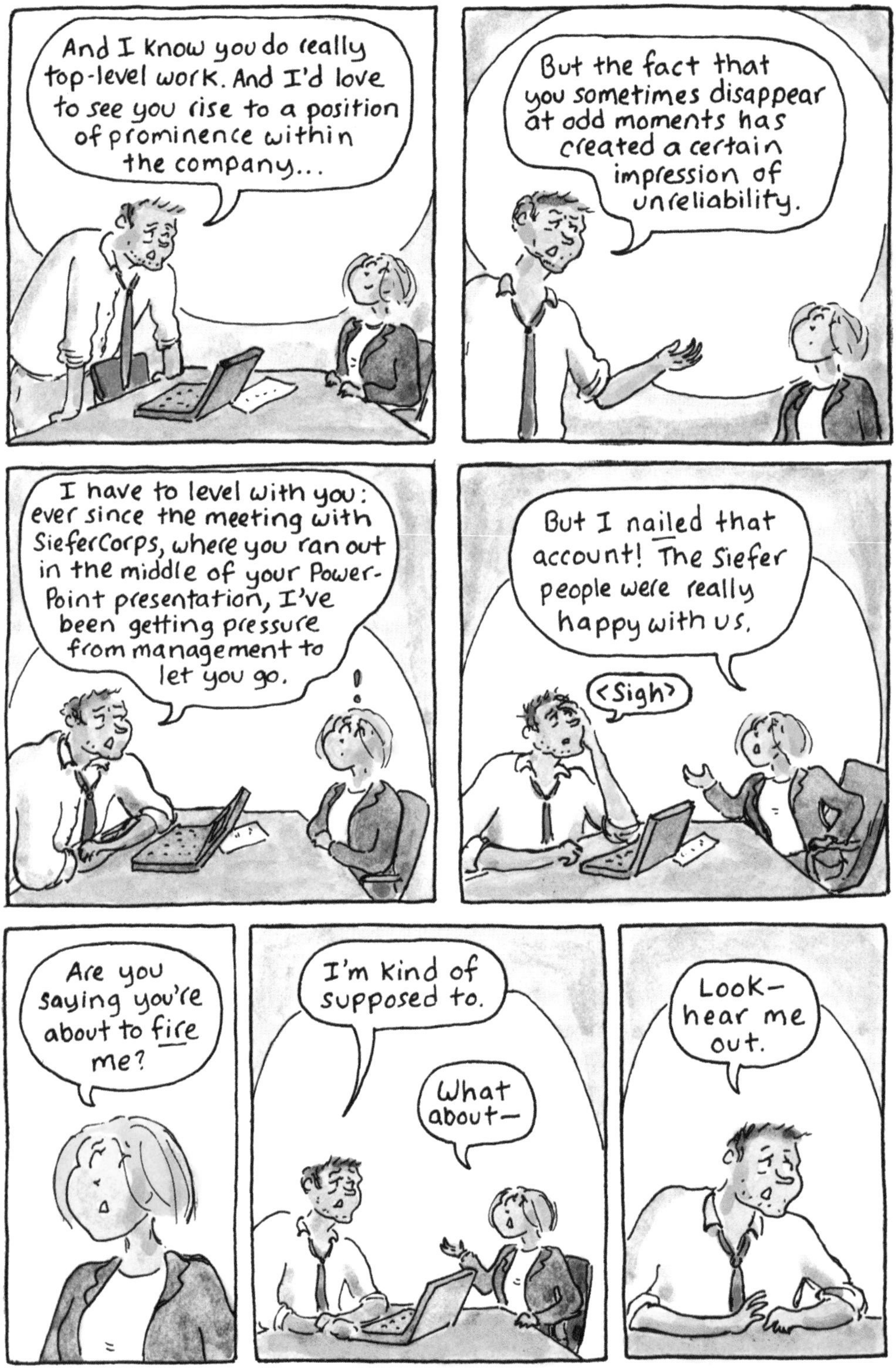
And I know you do really top-level work. And I'd love to see you rise to a position of prominence within the company...
But the fact that you sometimes disappear at odd moments has created a certain impression of unreliability.
I have to level with you: ever since the meeting with SieferCorps, where you ran out in the middle of your Power-Point presentation, I've been getting pressure from management to let you go.
!
But I nailed that account! The Siefer people were really happy with us.
<Sigh>
Are you saying you're about to fire me?
I'm kind of supposed to.
What about—
Look—hear me out.

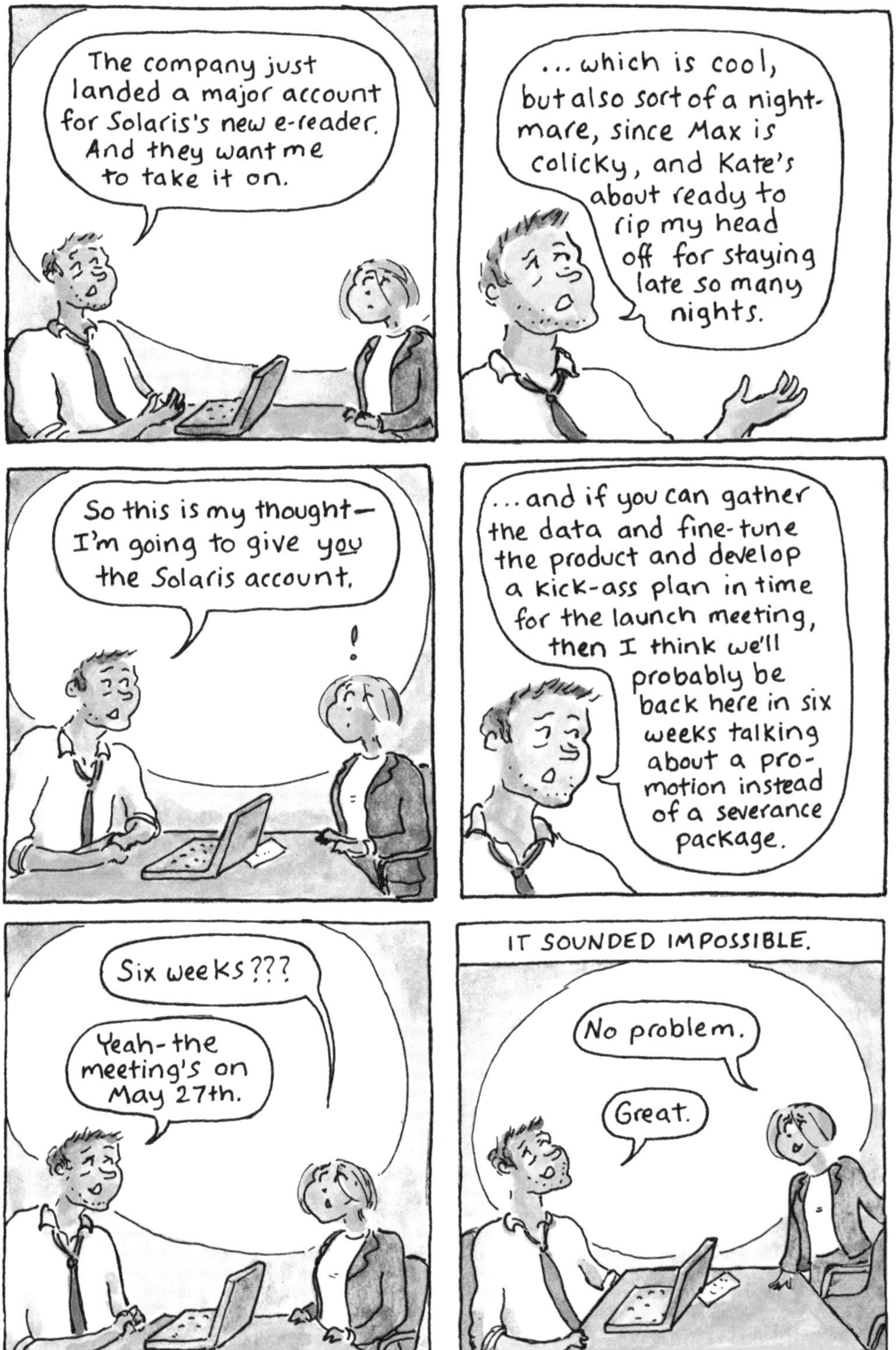
The company just landed a major account for Solaris's new e-reader. And they want me to take it on.
...which is cool, but also sort of a night-mare, since Max is colicky, and Kate's about ready to rip my head off for staying late so many nights.
So this is my thought— I'm going to give you the Solaris account.
!
...and if you can gather the data and fine-tune the product and develop a kick-ass plan in time for the launch meeting, then I think we'll probably be back here in six weeks talking about a pro-motion instead of a severance package.
Six weeks???
Yeah-the meeting's on May 27th.
IT SOUNDED IMPOSSIBLE.
No problem.
Great.

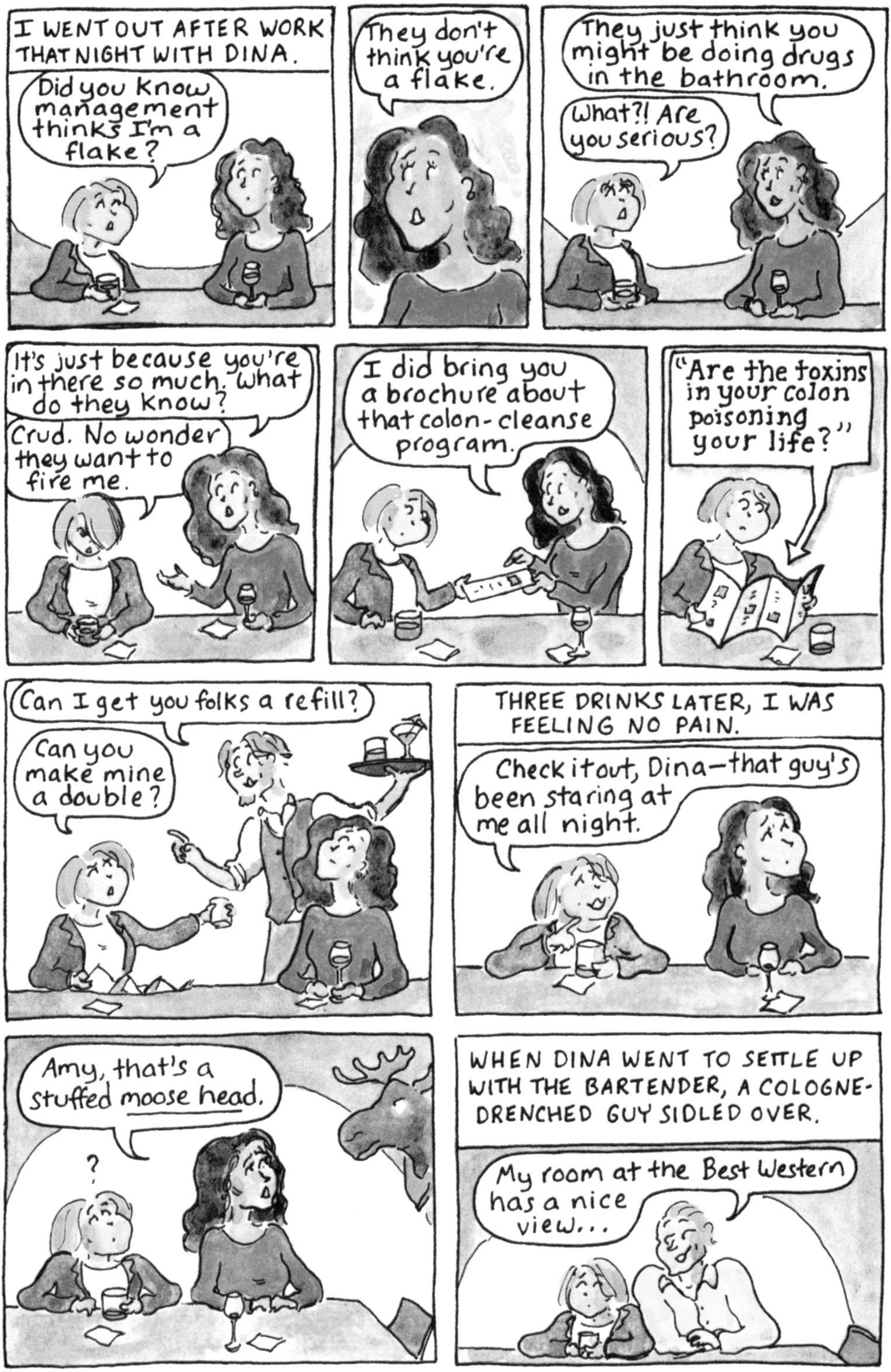
I WENT OUT AFTER WORK THAT NIGHT WITH DINA.
Did you know management thinks I'm a flake?
They don't think you're a flake.
They just think you might be doing drugs in the bathroom.
What?! Are you serious?
It's just because you're in there so much. What do they know?
Crud. No wonder they want to fire me.
I did bring you a brochure about that colon-cleanse program.
"Are the toxins in your colon poisoning your life?"
Can I get you folks a refill?
Can you make mine a double?
THREE DRINKS LATER, I WAS FEELING NO PAIN.
Check it out, Dina—that guy's been staring at me all night.
Amy, that's a stuffed moose head.
?
WHEN DINA WENT TO SETTLE UP WITH THE BARTENDER, A COLOGNE-DRENCHED GUY SIDLED OVER.
My room at the Best Western has a nice view...

...if you want to come check it out.

Does it have a bathroom?

'Cause I really have to pee.

Only the nicest bathroom in the city...

...for you, my little chiquita.

PINCH

I WAS KIND OF FUZZY ON WHAT HAPPENED NEXT...

POW

...BUT HE SEEMED TO BE NO LONGER STANDING IN FRONT OF ME.

Holy...she just dropped that guy like a tenpin!

Ok, we're all set with the—

What's with that guy?

Hmph?

He looksh shleepy.

DINA FETCHED ME A WATER AND HUSTLED ME INTO A CAB.

BY THE TIME I STUMBLED INTO BED, IT WAS 2:00 A.M.

BUT TWO HOURS LATER, MY EMERGENCY BUZZER WENT OFF.

I WAS HOVERING SOME-WHERE BETWEEN STILL DRUNK AND HUNGOVER.

Unghmph

I GAVE UP ON FIGURING OUT HOW TO GET INTO MY STRETCHY LITTLE OUTFIT...

Crud.

...AND THREW ON SWEATS INSTEAD.

RAIDERS

ALERT: Mugging spree in progress— Sutton Ave.

AS DISPLAYS OF VIGILANTE JUSTICE GO, IT WASN'T MY FINEST HOUR.

This guy *wasn't* mugging you?

No!

Sorry!— Tell him to put ice on it.

BY THE TIME I FOUND THE REAL MUGGER, HE WAS GOING AFTER HIS NEXT VICTIM.

Put the gun down!

What? Who the hell are you?

Drop the gun!

Screw tha—

ZZZTT

Starling???

RAIDERS

THE SUDDEN MOVE HAD UNSETTLED MY HUNGOVER STOMACH.

bleghghgh

!

Holy crap. You threw up on me!

I'm aware of that.

MY HEADACHE WAS HORRENDOUS.

RAIDERS

I need you to give him back his wallet now.

RAIDERS

Take it!

RAIDERS

I BROUGHT THE MUGGER TO THE POLICE STATION, WHERE THE ON-DUTY DETECTIVE RECOVERED FOUR MORE WALLETS FROM HIS COAT.

RAIDERS

FINALLY, AS THE SUN ROSE, I DRAGGED MY HUNGOVER SELF HOMEWARD ON FOOT, NOT WANTING TO RISK LOSING THE CONTENTS OF MY STOMACH ONTO THE HEADS OF UNSUSPECTING COMMUTERS.

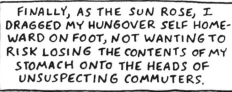

RAIDERS

ON RILEY STREET I HEARD A FAMILIAR VOICE.

Amy?!

Crud.

RAIDER

Russell.

How's it going?

RAIDER

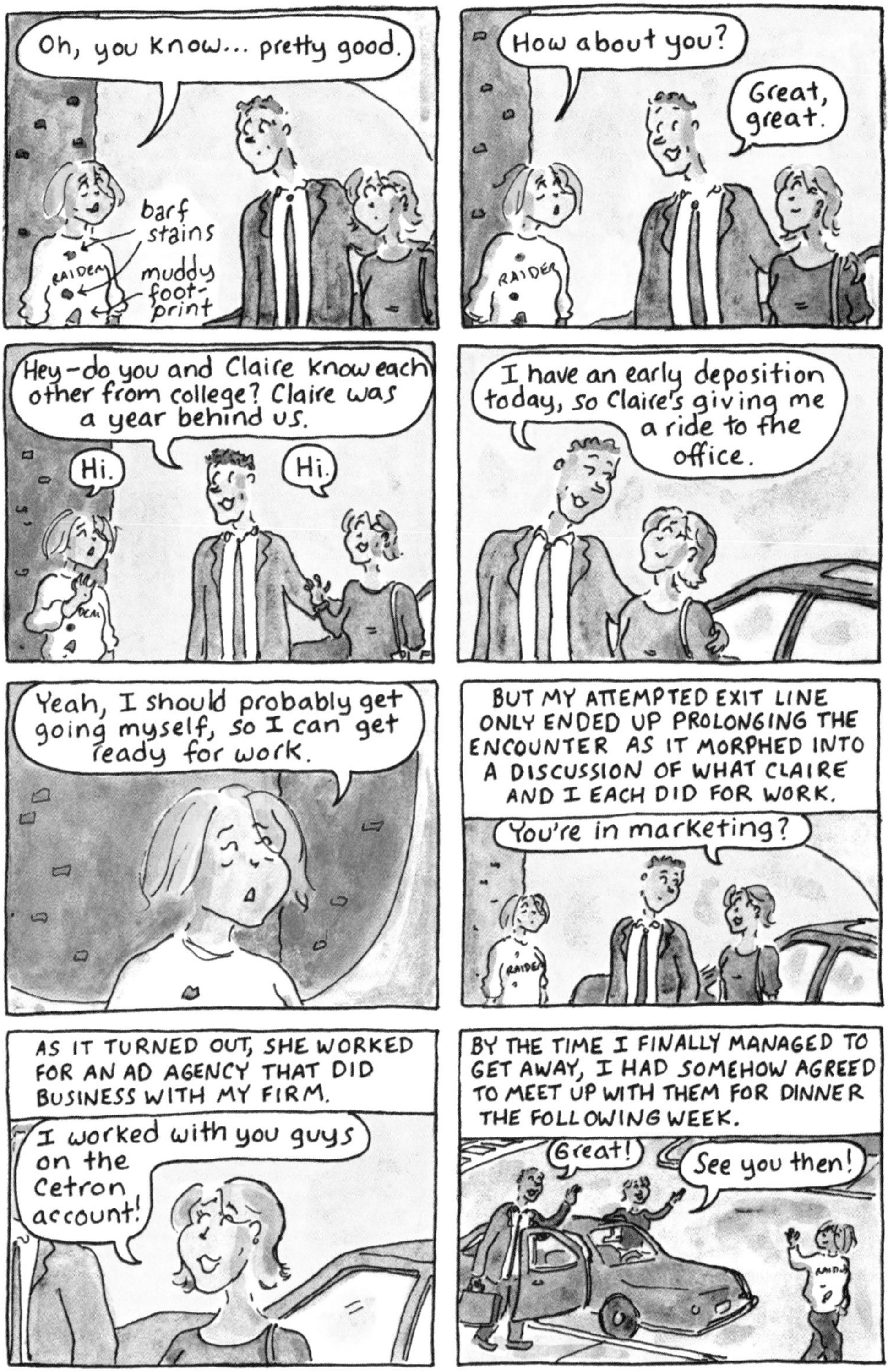
Oh, you know... pretty good.
barf stains
RAIDER
muddy foot-print
How about you?
Great, great.
RAIDER
Hey–do you and Claire know each other from college? Claire was a year behind us.
Hi.
Hi.
I have an early deposition today, so Claire's giving me a ride to the office.
Yeah, I should probably get going myself, so I can get ready for work.
BUT MY ATTEMPTED EXIT LINE ONLY ENDED UP PROLONGING THE ENCOUNTER AS IT MORPHED INTO A DISCUSSION OF WHAT CLAIRE AND I EACH DID FOR WORK.
You're in marketing?
RAIDER
AS IT TURNED OUT, SHE WORKED FOR AN AD AGENCY THAT DID BUSINESS WITH MY FIRM.
I worked with you guys on the Cetron account!
BY THE TIME I FINALLY MANAGED TO GET AWAY, I HAD SOMEHOW AGREED TO MEET UP WITH THEM FOR DINNER THE FOLLOWING WEEK.
Great!
See you then!

You have a date with your ex-boyfriend and his girlfriend?

It's not a date. And it's not like he was ever my boyfriend.

It still seems like a terrible idea.

His girlfriend, Claire, was all gung ho about it.

That's even weirder.

Well, she doesn't know about my almost-thing with Russell. And she's all excited to talk shop, because it turns out she's a creative director at Wallensby.

Wait—Wallensby? Are you talking about Claire Hayes?

Yeah, why?

I know Claire. She did work for us on the Cetron account!

Really? How was she?

THIS WAS SUPPOSED TO BE HER CUE FOR A SNARKY COMMENT.

She's awesome! You'll love her.

Great.

WITH THE E-READER ACCOUNT HANGING OVER MY HEAD, AT LEAST I HAD PLENTY TO TAKE MY MIND OFF MY LAME PERSONAL LIFE.

I THREW MYSELF INTO READING UP ON THE FIELD...

...STUDIED EVERY MODEL I COULD GET MY HANDS ON...

...AND WORKED SO LATE A FEW NIGHTS THAT I DIDN'T EVEN BOTHER TO GO HOME.

BUT WHEN DINNER NIGHT WITH RUSSELL AND CLAIRE ROLLED AROUND, I DUCKED OUT EARLY TO MAKE MYSELF LOOK SPIFFY.

...AND (CHEMICALLY, AT LEAST) TO APPROXIMATE SOME LEVEL OF CALM.

Xanax

AT THE APPOINTED HOUR, I JOINED RUSSELL AND CLAIRE AT THE BISTRO NEAR MY APARTMENT.

TO MY SURPRISE, THINGS WENT REMARKABLY WELL.

Oh my God — you had Professor Meyer, too? Didn't she make you feel like the biggest idiot?

Yeah, pretty much.

CLAIRE WAS REALLY NICE.

If you want, I can show you the new database-management program our office is using. It's actually not bad.

WE EVEN GOT TO TALKING ABOUT THE E-READER PROJECT, AND CLAIRE HAD SOME HELPFUL IDEAS.

What about a print campaign with a close-up, like this... and then the tagline here?

That's really good.

MEANWHILE, I WAS ACUTELY CON-SCIOUS OF RUSSELL AT MY ELBOW.

...STILL CUTE IN HIS GANGLY WAY.

I'D MADE SURE TO SIT WITH HIM ON MY GOOD SIDE, AND MADE A CONCERTED EFFORT TO KEEP MY HAIR UNDER CONTROL.

HE DID SEEM TO BE IN A REMINISCING MOOD.

Do you still have that wig you wore for the Marie Antoinette skit? That was hilarious.

WHEN WE SAID OUR GOOD-BYES, CLAIRE ENTHUSIASTICALLY SHOOK MY HAND.

I can sketch out some of those e-reader ad concepts for you.

Thanks!

RUSSELL WAS HARDER TO READ.

Hey, good to catch up.

BUT I THOUGHT MAYBE HE HUNG ON TO MY HAND A FRACTION LONGER THAN NECESSARY.

...OR SO I HOPED.

THE NEXT DAY AT WORK, MY CONFIDENCE SOARED WHEN I SAW THE POSTER DINA'S NEW ASSISTANT, SAM, HAD TAPED TO HIS CUBICLE.

This is yours?

Yeah—I'm a huge Starling fan.

Really.

Are you kidding?

She totally kicks butt.

She does, doesn't she?

Who, Starling? Isn't she kind of a spaz, though?

No.

You mean because she forgets her belt and cape sometimes?

Yeah—that and because in the news photos she always kind of looks like she didn't bother to brush her hair— or she's trying to hold it back with, like, rubber bands and binder clips or something.

It probably gets messed up from flying.

And I saw in the Tribune last week that she took some guy down by throwing up on him.

Maybe she just wasn't feeling well.

And she was drunk and wearing sweat pants.

Touché...

WHEN MY NEXT EMERGENCY CALL CAME IN THAT NIGHT, I PROCRASTINATED EVEN LONGER THAN USUAL.

Belt ☑
Boots ☑
Mask
Gloves
Cape ☐

ALERT: Suspicious activity— Animal Rescue League roof.

I SWOOPED IN WITH A FLOURISH.

Hold it right there!

THE TWO GUYS ON THE ROOF DIDN'T SEEM ESPECIALLY APPRECIATIVE OF THE EXTRA EFFORT I'D MADE WITH MY APPEARANCE.

Please! Don't throw up on us—these are our only clothes!

I threw up on one person, once, by accident!

I GOT THEM BOTH BY THE COLLAR.

OK—spit it out! What are you lowlifes doing up here?

I COULD FEEL THEM SHAKING.

I WAS STARTING TO FEEL LIKE KIND OF A JERK.

FINALLY ONE OF THEM STARTED SPLUTTERING.

Bobby only came along because I talked him into it.

Into what?

Getting my dog.

Your dog's in here?

Yeah—the animal control guy said he shouldn't be living with a homeless person.

So you were just going to break in and take him?

I WRENCHED OFF THE SKYLIGHT AND DRAGGED THE GUY DOWN INTO THE BUILDING WITH ME.

HE LOOKED LIKE HE THOUGHT I WAS ABOUT TO MURDER HIM IN THE DOG RUN.

So you claim one of these mutts is yours?

ACTUALLY, HE DIDN'T HAVE TO TELL ME.

Sparky!

IT WAS A SHAME I'D PUT ON ALL THAT EYE MAKEUP.

THESE DAYS, IT SEEMED I WAS DOING A BETTER JOB ABETTING CRIMES THAN THWARTING THEM.

TWO DAYS LATER, WHEN I GOT HOME FROM WORK, I COULD SEE A PAIR OF LEGS WAITING FOR ME AT THE TOP OF THE STAIRS.

FOR A MOMENT, I DARED TO HOPE IT WAS RUSSELL, COME TO DECLARE HIS UNDYING AFFECTIONS.

BUT NO...

...ACTUALLY...

...EVEN BETTER.

Noah!

MY ELUSIVE LITTLE BROTHER, WHO I HADN'T SEEN IN OVER A YEAR, WAS ON MY DOORSTEP.

Long time no see!

Hey, sis.

OTHER THAN DR. MORRIS, NOAH WAS THE ONLY PERSON WHO KNEW ABOUT MY FREAKISH POWERS.

WE DIDN'T REALLY TALK ABOUT IT, THOUGH.

WHEN HE WAS LITTLE, AND I'D FIRST GOTTEN MY STARLING SUIT, HE'D DOWNRIGHT WORSHIPPED ME.

Do another one!

IT THRILLED HIM WHEN I TOLD HIM HIS OWN POWERS WOULD KICK IN WHEN HE WAS A TEENAGER.

...and then you can beat up anybody.

I ASSUMED I WAS DOING HIM A FAVOR: I WISHED SOMEONE HAD GIVEN ME FAIR WARNING.

BUT HIS ADOLESCENCE CAME AND WENT WITH NO SPECIAL POWERS.

Ow! #@!★

AND EVEN THOUGH HE WAS STILL AS SWEET AS EVER, IT WAS CLEAR HIS LACK OF POWERS FELT LIKE A FAILURE TO HIM, AND HE STARTED DOING STUPID STUFF AND GETTING IN TROUBLE.

EMERGENCY EXIT

MY PARENTS WERE SO PREOCCUPIED WITH THEIR GIANT CAT COLONY THEY HARDLY NOTICED THEIR SON WAS SPENDING ALMOST AS MUCH TIME IN SUSPENSION AS IN SCHOOL.

Would you help me get Mr. Whiskers out of the chimney?

Yeah, sure.

HE WAS SMART, AND SHOULD HAVE BEEN IN COLLEGE, BUT I WAS PRETTY SURE HE'D SKIPPED SO MANY CLASSES HE'D NEVER EVEN GRADUATED FROM HIGH SCHOOL.

HE GENERALLY FOUND ODD JOBS AND FRIENDS TO LIVE WITH, AND DISAPPEARED FOR LONG STRETCHES DOING WHO KNOWS WHAT.

You want to stay here?

Is that ok?

Of course.

So what are you up to these days?

Different stuff.

I have a part-time security guard job, and I help some guys out moving stuff.

Sounds good.

AT LEAST IT WAS BETTER THAN THE YEAR HE TRIED PLAYING UPSIDE-DOWN BUCKETS IN THE SUBWAY FOR A LIVING.

I HUMMED WHILE I GOT THE COUCH SET UP FOR HIM.

IT WAS NICE TO HAVE COMPANY.

AT WORK, THE E-READER PROJECT WAS STILL RUNNING ME RAGGED.

DINA HELPFULLY BROUGHT SANDWICHES BACK FROM MY FAVORITE DELI EVERY DAY SO I WOULDN'T HAVE TO TAKE TIME TO RUN OUT MYSELF.

Special delivery!

ACROSS THE HALL, JASON WAS CLEARLY STRUGGLING WITH THE HEALTHMARK ACCOUNT.

?

BUT HE KNEW BETTER THAN TO ASK ME FOR HELP.

BY THE TIME I GOT HOME, IT WAS USUALLY LATE, AND I WAS FRAZZLED AND WIPED OUT.

BUT HAVING NOAH AROUND PERKED ME BACK UP.

Yo, what's happening?

THE NIGHTS HE WAS HOME, HE WOULD WAIT TO HAVE HIS DINNER WITH ME.

Remember that time you laughed so hard a chicken McNugget came out your nose?

Shut up—that was gross.

WE WATCHED JUNK TV.

No, you're the one who's drunk!

AND SOMETIMES WE WENT AROUND THE CORNER FOR ICE CREAM.

Do you think Dad even likes cats?

Has it ever really been relevant what Dad likes?

SOMETIMES I COULD EVEN GET HIM TO HELP ME WITH MY RESEARCH FOR WORK.

Ok, I plotted the data.

Cool.

IT BUGGED ME: HE WAS WAY TOO SMART TO BE SPENDING HIS LIFE BUMMING AROUND LIKE THIS.

TUESDAY MORNING, I GOT AN UNEXPECTED PHONE CALL.

Hey, Amy— It's Russell.

Claire made some proposed ad mock-ups for you. She was going to messenger them over, but it turns out I have a meeting over your way, so I could bring them by.

Uh, thanks.

WE ARRANGED TO MEET FOR LUNCH.

Russell (?!)
12:30

Hey, Russell.

Amy...

BETWEEN BITES OF OUR SANDWICHES, WE CHATTED AWKWARDLY ABOUT LIFE SINCE COLLEGE.

...so the commute's actually pretty easy.

That's good.

IT WAS ONLY WHEN WE WERE ALMOST DONE, AND I'D HANDED HIM HALF MY CHOCOLATE CHIP COOKIE, THAT WE FINALLY GOT PAST THE SMALL TALK.

You know, it always kind of bummed me out the way you just disappeared senior year.

Yeah, I know— that was lame.

I wondered if maybe I did something that bothered you.

No, it was just my own stupid reasons.

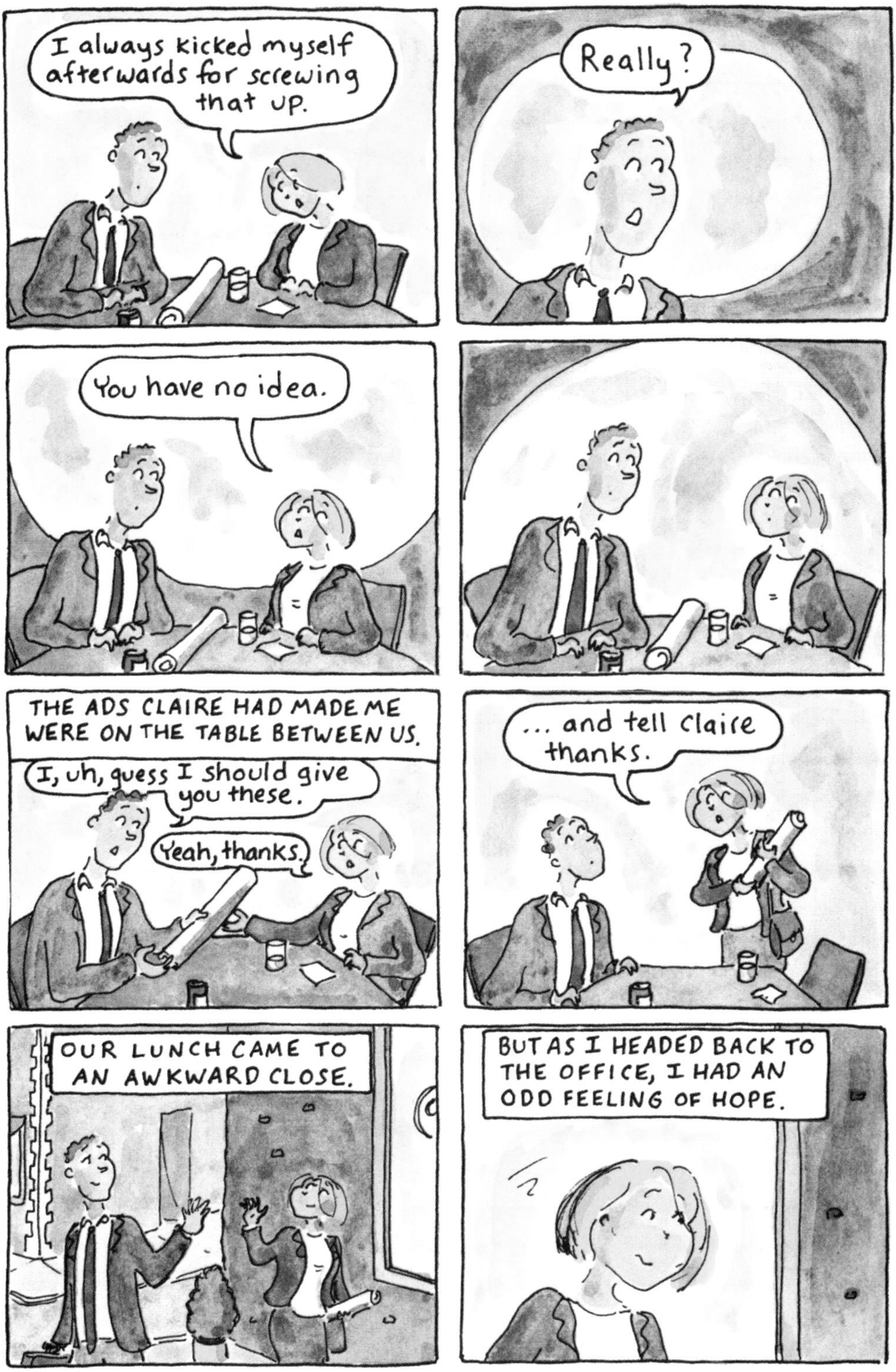
I always kicked myself afterwards for screwing that up.
Really?
You have no idea.
THE ADS CLAIRE HAD MADE ME WERE ON THE TABLE BETWEEN US.
I, uh, guess I should give you these.
Yeah, thanks.
... and tell claire thanks.
OUR LUNCH CAME TO AN AWKWARD CLOSE.
BUT AS I HEADED BACK TO THE OFFICE, I HAD AN ODD FEELING OF HOPE.

BACK AT THE DESK, I PULLED OUT CLAIRE'S MOCK-UPS.

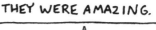
THEY WERE AMAZING.

SHE WAS CLEARLY INCREDIBLY TALENTED, AND THESE WERE INSPIRED.

IT SOLVED A MAJOR PIECE OF THE PUZZLE FOR ME IN TERMS OF MY LONG CHECKLIST FOR THE E-READER MARKETING PLAN.

Prototype
Focus group
Print + Web ad campaigns
Data analysis
Presc...

I COULDN'T RESIST CALLING CLAIRE RIGHT AWAY.

Claire—these ideas are awesome! I'm definitely including them in the proposal.

Oh, excellent! Thank you so much!

So if Solaris goes for them, can we contract with you to cover the print advertising angle?

I would love that. Thank you!

THANKS TO RUSSELL—AND NOW CLAIRE—FOR ONCE I WAS HAVING A GOOD DAY.

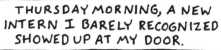

Do you have a minute?

I REALLY DIDN'T.

If it's something you can shoot me an email about, that would be great.

Actually, it's kind of personal.

MY CURIOSITY GOT THE BETTER OF ME, AND I INVITED HER IN.

I was, uh, wondering if you could recommend a clinic.

A what?

You know— like a medical facility that deals with things confidentially.

Deals with what things?

You know— the, uh... I have the same issue as you.

I WAS FLOORED. DID SHE HAVE FREAKISH POWERS, TOO?

You do?

Yeah, kind of a bummer, huh?

Wow, I never expected to meet someone else in my situa- tion.

Well, herpes isn't all that uncommon, really. But it's true that most people—

Herpes?!

I MARCHED OVER TO FIND HIM, HANDS SPARKING.

BUT MADDENINGLY, BEFORE I COULD TRACK HIM DOWN AND THROTTLE HIM... MY BUZZER WENT OFF.

I MUTTERED ANGRILY THE WHOLE WAY OVER.

JUST AS I ARRIVED AT THE BRIDGE, A FIGURE DROPPED OVER THE SIDE.

I HAD TO PICK UP SPEED TO CATCH HER.

Oof.

IRRITATINGLY, SHE WAS LESS THAN APPRECIATIVE.

Finally I get the nerve to jump, and you show up and catch me?!

You want me to put you back up there?

I thought you were supposed to talk me out of this.

Not today. I'm in a worse mood than you are.

I ENDED UP FLYING HER ALL THE WAY TO HER APARTMENT, THREE TOWNS OVER.

BY THE TIME WE GOT THERE, I HAD NO IDEA WHY SHE'D JUMPED, BUT SHE WAS GIVING ME A VIGOROUS PEP TALK.

I'm telling you — guy wants to spread dirty rumors about you, you give him herpes for real.

Yeah, well, the point is that I don't actually have herpes, so that's not really an option.

Oh, yeah? I got herpes. You give me his name, I'll take care of him.

I TOOK DOWN HER PHONE NUMBER JUST IN CASE.

BY THE TIME I GOT BACK TO THE OFFICE, I WAS RUNNING LATE.

I'D FINALLY MANAGED TO GET ENOUGH PARTICIPANTS SIGNED UP FOR AN E-READER FOCUS GROUP.

Bob Cole
Samantha Roy
Kim Crane
Paul Kahn
Ellen D'Angelo
Lee Ha...

BUT IT WAS SCHEDULED FOR 2 P.M., AND ALREADY IT WAS A COUPLE MINUTES AFTER.

I RACED TO THE CONFERENCE ROOM.

BUT WHEN I FLUNG OPEN THE DOORS, NOBODY WAS THERE.

?!

What the—?

FINALLY I FOUND A NEARBY SECRETARY.

Yeah, there were a bunch of people here, but Jason came by and said the focus group was cancelled.

Was that bad?

I TRIED CALLING THE PARTICIPANTS BACK.

I'm sorry about the misunderstanding.

BUT ALREADY, THEY WERE HALFWAY BACK TO THEIR JOBS AND HOMES—AND MORE THAN A LITTLE ANNOYED.

No, I'm afraid I can't re-schedule.

I skipped an important meeting to be there this afternoon.

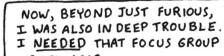
NOW, BEYOND JUST FURIOUS, I WAS ALSO IN DEEP TROUBLE. I __NEEDED__ THAT FOCUS GROUP DATA ASAP.

JASON — WISELY — SEEMED TO BE MAKING HIMSELF SCARCE.

I FOUND DINA INSTEAD.

You available for emergency drinks?

Sure thing.

He's so evil — I don't understand what his problem is.

He's just a creep.

You know, Sam said he saw Jason snooping around your desk today while you were out.

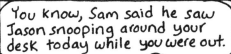

Are you __serious__?!

I think he's freaked-out that you're going to have some big success with the e-reader and get promoted over his head.

But what's the point of snooping around my office? That's just creepy.

I don't know. Knowing him, he's probably hoping to steal your ideas and suggest them himself or something.

Great. Why does Dan pay no attention to any of this?

Dan? He's useless these days. He comes in every morning half-asleep and covered in spit-up.

True.

...which is why you need to tell him. In the state he's in, it's not like he's going to pick up on this stuff himself.

Yeah, but if I go running to Dan and say Jason's sabotaging me, you know Jason's just going to make up some story that makes me sound even worse.

I'm on thin enough ice as it is.

Fine. But if you're going to be all Lone Ranger about it, at least watch your back.

...Don't let Jason within ten feet of the work you're doing on the e-reader.

ON MY WAY HOME, I BOUGHT A PADLOCK FOR MY DESK DRAWER.

BOLT-SAFE

WHEN I FINALLY GOT TO BED, I THOROUGHLY ZONKED OUT.

BUT EVEN THEN, MY DAY WASN'T OVER.

ALERT: Theft in progress—Norwood Art Museum

AT LEAST I WAS GETTING SUMMONED SOMEPLACE NICE FOR A CHANGE.

NORWOOD ART MUSEUM

BUT IT WAS MAINLY JUST CREEPY AT NIGHT.

AND I'D OBVIOUSLY PROCRASTINATED A LITTLE TOO LONG: THE THIEF WAS NOWHERE IN SIGHT.

I FINALLY FOUND TWO GUARDS LOCKED IN THE CONTROL ROOM.

We sat down in here to play canasta, and some guy slammed the door and locked us in.

A PAIR OF POLICE DETECTIVES ARRIVED JUST BEHIND ME.

Do we know what he took?

We could see on the cameras. It was a painting from the pile of stuff waiting to go up in the Edgy and Emerging exhibit.

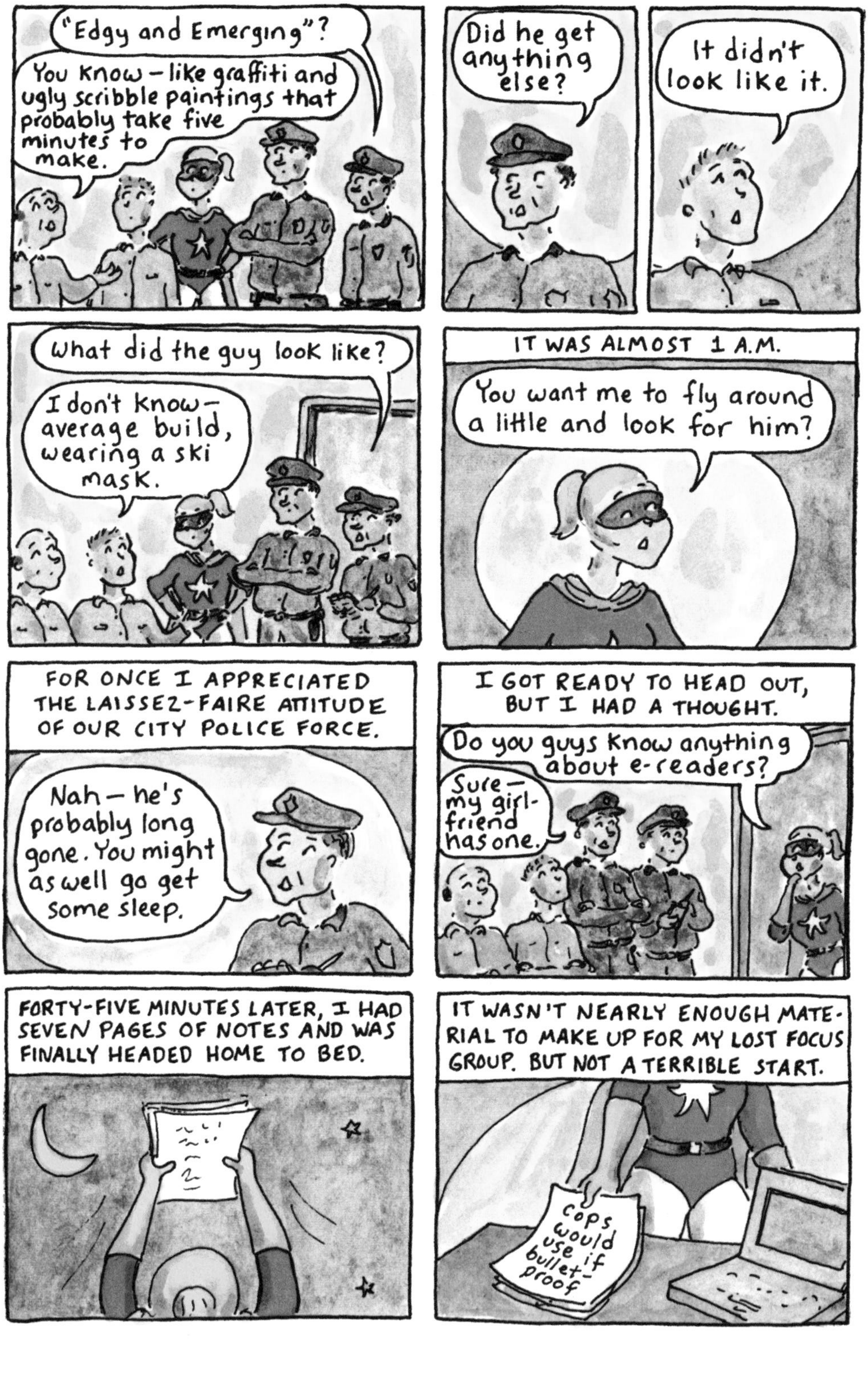

"Edgy and Emerging"?
You know—like graffiti and ugly scribble paintings that probably take five minutes to make.
Did he get anything else?
It didn't look like it.
What did the guy look like?
I don't know—average build, wearing a ski mask.
IT WAS ALMOST 1 A.M.
You want me to fly around a little and look for him?
FOR ONCE I APPRECIATED THE LAISSEZ-FAIRE ATTITUDE OF OUR CITY POLICE FORCE.
Nah—he's probably long gone. You might as well go get some sleep.
I GOT READY TO HEAD OUT, BUT I HAD A THOUGHT.
Do you guys know anything about e-readers?
Sure—my girlfriend has one.
FORTY-FIVE MINUTES LATER, I HAD SEVEN PAGES OF NOTES AND WAS FINALLY HEADED HOME TO BED.
IT WASN'T NEARLY ENOUGH MATERIAL TO MAKE UP FOR MY LOST FOCUS GROUP. BUT NOT A TERRIBLE START.
cops would use if bullet-proof

WHEN I PASSED JASON IN THE HALL THE NEXT DAY, HE SMILED INNOCENTLY AT ME.

I JUST CLENCHED MY TEETH AND SMILED COLDLY BACK.

TO MY SURPRISE, THE EFFECT ON HIM WAS RATHER GRATIFYING.

SATURDAY NIGHT, NOAH AND I SETTLED IN TO WATCH '70s HORROR NIGHT ON CABLE.

THE WEREWOLF OF WOODSTOCK WAS JUST ABOUT TO WRAP UP WHEN MY BUZZER WENT OFF.

crud.

ALERT:
Brawl:
warehouse behind Sciarpo's Market.

AS USUAL, I PROCRASTINATED.

Aren't you going to be late?

<sigh> Tell me what happens.

I HATED BRAWLS—THEY USUALLY MEANT HAVING TO TAKE DOWN MULTIPLE PEOPLE AT ONCE, WHICH MEANT I'D BE TWICE AS SORE IN THE MORNING.

AS I CLOSED IN ON THE BACK LOT OF THE WAREHOUSE DISTRICT, I COULD SEE A MASS OF GUYS WRESTLING AND WRANGLING BELOW.

BUT THE MOMENT I DROPPED TO THE GROUND, THEY STEPPED AWAY FROM EACH OTHER AND TURNED TO LOOK AT ME.

Are you people having a problem?

NOTHING...

I WAS GETTING NERVOUS.

What the...?

FINALLY, AN IMPOSING GUY FROM THE BACK STEPPED FORWARD.

I needed to talk to you.

This was the only way I could think of to do it.

I WAS ANNOYED.

Look— if there's not an actual problem here, I'll just be on my way.

Please— there is a problem.

I run a gambling business. And yeah, I know that's not—

NOW I WAS REALLY ANNOYED.

A gambling business? Sorry— I'm not in the business of facilitating criminal pursuits.

I TURNED TO GO.

Really? So you didn't steal a dog for a homeless guy from the Animal Rescue League?

...or let a couple of bank robbers go— with a pile of cash?

I know people. Things get around.

I thought you might be willing to help me.

My business doesn't hurt anyone. We run bets and wagering games for people — that's it.

But these guys from the east side have infiltrated my organization and they're running drugs and dealing to my patrons.

WHEREVER HE WAS GOING WITH THIS WAS SO NOT MY PROBLEM.

I need to clean house. I'm a fighter; I can throw my weight around. But these guys are bad news. I can't do it myself.

<Sigh> Look, even if I wanted to spend my spare time fighting armed drug dealers, unfortunately for you, I don't have any spare time.

I thought you cared about this city.

Sorry to disappoint you.

I GOT READY TO TAKE OFF.

You don't by any chance have a moment to answer a few questions about e-readers, do you?

SURVEY

FROM THE LOOK ON HIS FACE, I DEDUCED THAT HE DID NOT.

?!

SURVEY

SUNDAY I HAD TO GO TO A BRIDAL SHOWER FOR DINA.

IT WAS ONE OF THOSE EVENTS WITH QUICHE AND FLOWERY DRESSES AND TASTEFUL GIFTS.

Those napkin rings are gorgeous!

...EXCEPT, OF COURSE, FOR MINE.

Did you register for that?

I'D PICKED IT UP ON MY WAY HOME THE PREVIOUS NIGHT.

NO TRESPASSING
Demolition Site

DINA LIKED IT AT LEAST.

This is awesome!

I WAS SURPRISED TO SEE THAT CLAIRE WAS THERE, TOO.

I'D FORGOTTEN THAT SHE AND DINA WERE FRIENDS THROUGH WORK.

Hey, how are things going with the e-reader?

Ugh... don't ask.

That good, huh?

This jerk Jason at work keeps deliberately screwing things up for her.

Jason Treadway?

How did you know?

I did ads with him on the Rizzo account. Yeah—he's awful: he's like a weird mix of incompetent and calcu-lating.

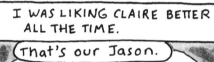

I WAS LIKING CLAIRE BETTER ALL THE TIME.

That's our Jason.

Well, if you need help with anything—like mock-ups for presentations or whatever, just let me know.

IT WAS NICE OF HER TO OFFER.

Thanks.

BUT THE LAST THING I NEEDED WAS TO WIND UP EVEN MORE INDEBTED TO THE GIRL WHOSE BOYFRIEND I COULDN'T HELP WANTING TO STEAL.

EVEN FREE-SPIRIT NOAH THOUGHT I WAS BEING LAME.

She's saving your ass at work. You can't just put the moves on her boyfriend.

I'm such a freak— it's not like anything would ever happen with him anyway.

Maybe you should try going out with old guys. At least if they have heart attacks, you can defibrillate them with your hands.

Shut up!

Ow.

AS I APPROACHED THE OFFICE TUESDAY MORNING, I ALMOST BUMPED INTO SOMEONE COMING AROUND THE CORNER.

Amy! How's it going?

Russell?

I was dropping something off for a client down the street. You want to join me for a cup of coffee?

THE LAST THING I NEEDED WAS A COFFEE BREAK BEFORE MY DAY EVEN STARTED. BUT NO WAY WAS I TURNING THIS DOWN.

Sure.

IT FELT WEIRDLY DATE-LIKE.

I got it— you have a seat.

OUR CONVERSATION FROM LAST TIME HUNG IN THE AIR BETWEEN US.

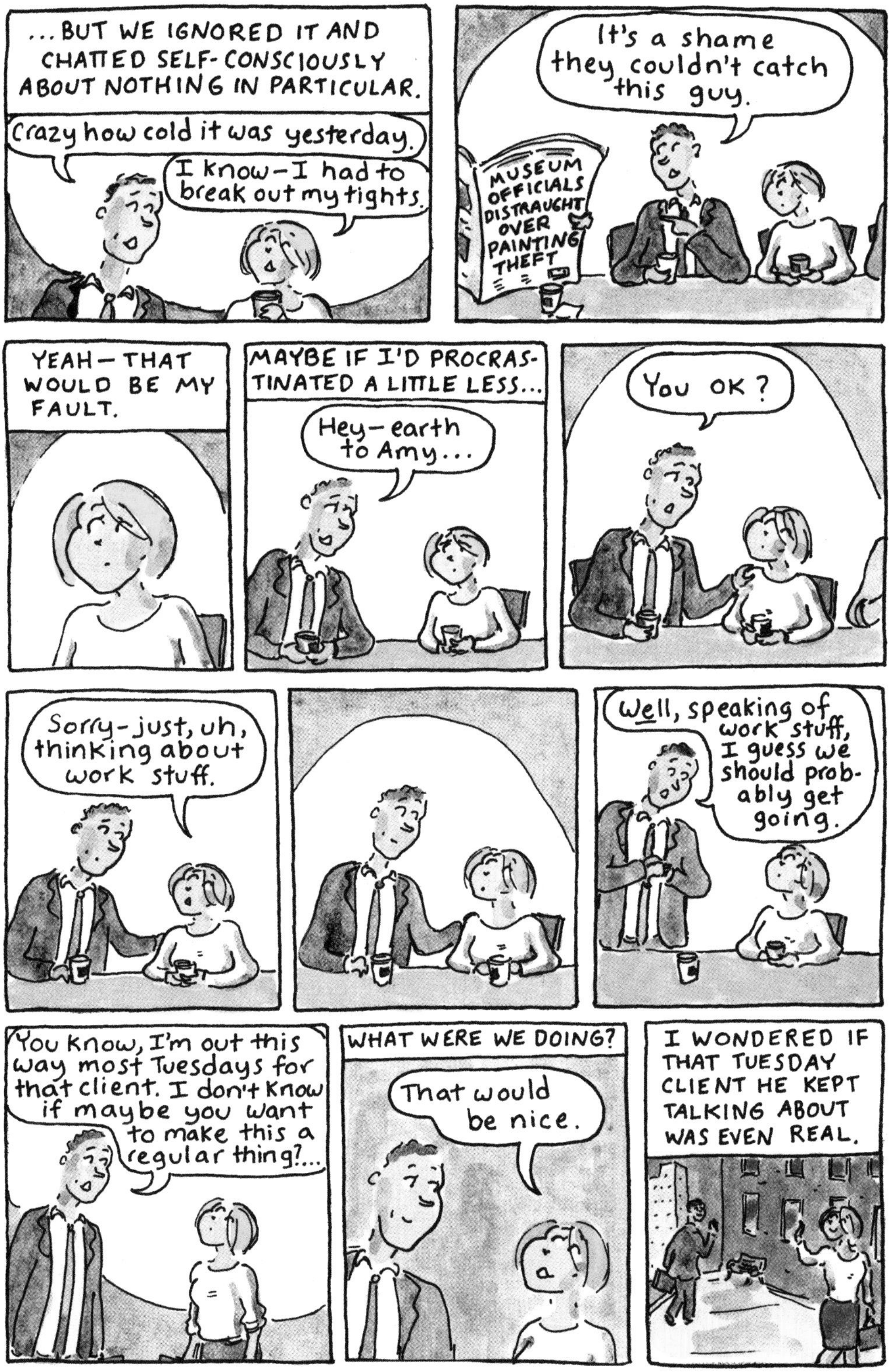

...BUT WE IGNORED IT AND CHATTED SELF-CONSCIOUSLY ABOUT NOTHING IN PARTICULAR.
Crazy how cold it was yesterday.
I know—I had to break out my tights.
It's a shame they couldn't catch this guy.
MUSEUM OFFICIALS DISTRAUGHT OVER PAINTING THEFT
YEAH—THAT WOULD BE MY FAULT.
MAYBE IF I'D PROCRASTINATED A LITTLE LESS...
Hey—earth to Amy...
You OK?
Sorry—just, uh, thinking about work stuff.
Well, speaking of work stuff, I guess we should probably get going.
You know, I'm out this way most Tuesdays for that client. I don't know if maybe you want to make this a regular thing?...
WHAT WERE WE DOING?
That would be nice.
I WONDERED IF THAT TUESDAY CLIENT HE KEPT TALKING ABOUT WAS EVEN REAL.

TWO NIGHTS LATER, I WAS SOUND ASLEEP WHEN MY BUZZER WENT OFF.

WHEN I SAW THE MESSAGE, I WAS MAJORLY ANNOYED.

ALERT:
Brawl—
Warehouse
behind
Sciarpo's
Market

IT WAS OBVIOUSLY THAT GAMBLER GUY AGAIN.

I TOOK MY TIME EVEN MORE THAN USUAL.

eMail

AS I APPROACHED, I COULD SEE GUYS WRANGLING, JUST LIKE LAST TIME.

I DROPPED TO LAND AND WAITED FOR THEM TO STOP LIKE LAST TIME, TOO.

BUT THEY KEPT ON FIGHTING.

?

Hello.

crud.

Xanax

I PLOWED INTO THE FRAY.

EVENTUALLY I TOOK TO INDISCRIMINATELY ZAPPING ANYONE I COULD GET MY HANDS ON.

A HUGE LUG OF A GUY FELL RIGHT ON TOP OF ME.

Oof.

I SHOOK HIM OFF AND STOOD UP.

THAT'S WHEN I SAW IT...

MY LITTLE BROTHER (?!!) — BACKED UP AGAINST A WALL, WITH SOME GUY POINTING A GUN AT HIM.

Noah!!

OUT OF NOWHERE, GAMBLER GUY APPEARED AND TACKLED THE GUY WITH THE GUN.

I WATCHED, SPEECHLESS, AS NOAH SCAMPERED AWAY.

I WANTED TO GO AFTER HIM.

BUT THERE WAS STILL WORK TO BE DONE TO GET THIS MESS UNDER CONTROL.

I PULLED OUT MY BEEPER TO SUMMON HELP.

POLICE BACKUP

No.

Wha...?

No police.

I WOULD HAVE TOLD HIM TO BUZZ OFF, BUT NOAH'S MYSTERIOUS IN-VOLVEMENT IN ALL THIS WAS WORRI-SOME. KEEPING LAW ENFORCEMENT AWAY UNTIL I COULD SORT OUT WHAT WAS GOING ON MAYBE WASN'T SUCH A BAD IDEA...

I'll help you.

OH, BROTHER...

Whatever. Just don't get in the way.

I GOT BACK TO WORK.

GAMBLER GUY ACTUALLY SEEMED TO BE DOING OK.

A HALF HOUR LATER, IT WAS JUST US AND A BUNCH OF STUNNED GUYS ON THE GROUND.

which of these guys are yours?

THE LAST THING I NEEDED WAS FOR THE TWO GROUPS TO WAKE UP AND START FIGHTING AGAIN.

I HELPED HIM DRAG HIS PEOPLE INSIDE.

THE ONES LEFT ON THE GROUND LOOKED PRETTY SEEDY.

Who are these guys?

Rex Daniels's people.

That's the drug gang?

Yup.

That guy Noah—how do you know him?

I'm assuming he's one of yours?

No.

?!

So how do you know hi—?

BUT I WAS DONE ANSWERING QUESTIONS.

I HIGHTAILED IT HOME TO TALK TO NOAH.

THE APARTMENT WAS EMPTY.

ZZZZZ

JUST BEFORE DAWN I HEARD THE DOOR.

What the hell, Noah?

What are you into?

Nothing.

Come on— I'm not stupid.

You're running drugs for Rex Daniels's people aren't you?

I told you I was helping people move stuff.

CRUD. I HAD SO WANTED TO BE WRONG.

Are you doing drugs, too?

Not anymore — no.

GREAT. NOT ANYMORE? WHAT ELSE DID I HAVE NO CLUE ABOUT?

This is so pathetic.

You're like fifty times smarter than half the people I deal with every day at work. Why don't you let me hook you up with an internship or something?

At least please quit whatever you're doing for Rex.

I almost saw you get shot tonight.

I was in the process of quitting anyway. I just need to talk to Rex.

I SAT AND WATCHED HIM SLEEP UNTIL I HAD TO GET READY FOR WORK.

NOAH DIDN'T COME HOME THE NEXT NIGHT.

...OR THE NIGHT AFTER THAT.

STILL, I WENT TO WORK.

I PLUGGED AWAY ON THE SOLARIS ACCOUNT...

I KEPT A WARY EYE ON JASON.

...AND EVEN MADE AN EMERGENCY RESCUE...

...WHILE HITTING UP WHOEVER I COULD FIND FOR E-READER FOCUS GROUP FEEDBACK.

BUT I WAS A MESS.

DINA'S ASSISTANT SEEMED TO HAVE ADDED TO HIS PORTRAIT GALLERY.

ONE OF THE PICTURES CAUGHT MY EYE.

Who's this guy?

Matt McRae. You don't watch Ultimate Fighting?

No—who's Matt McRae?

You know—UFC middleweight fighting champ? Don't you remember he took down that guy Fang in a big upset a couple years ago?

No.

He looks familiar, though.

He runs this big gambling operation now. You've probably seen him at Fight Club Wagerers.

Gambler guy?

Amy does not hang out in underground gambling clubs. She probably saw him when he was on The Tonight Show or something.

How underground can his club be, if everyone seems to know about it?

It probably doesn't need to be that underground. It's just gambling.

YEAH—AND APPARENTLY DRUGS AND BRAWLS, AND GUNS POINTED AT MY LITTLE BROTHER...

SATURDAY I SPENT THE MORNING CHECKING LOCAL NEWS REPORTS.

I WAS HALF-STRESSED, HALF-RELIEVED NOT TO FIND ANYTHING NOAH-RELATED.

No Results

AN EMAIL FROM RUSSELL MOMENTARILY BRIGHTENED MY MOOD.

Confirmed w/ client re. Tues. See you @ the Coffee House bright & early...;-)

BUT AN EMAIL FROM NOAH WOULD HAVE BEEN 20 TIMES BETTER.

MID-AFTERNOON THERE WAS A KNOCK ON THE DOOR.

I FLUNG IT OPEN, HOPING FOR NOAH.

37B

GAMBLER GUY?

37B

?!

Are you Amy Sturgess?

Who wants to know?

My name's Matt. I realize you don't know me, but I'm wondering if you might be familiar with someone named Noah?

Gulp

TERRIFIED ABOUT WHATEVER HE WAS COMING TO TELL ME, I USHERED HIM INSIDE.

37B

Is Noah your boyfriend?

Why are **you** asking about Noah?!

He seems to have gone missing.

No duh...

What ha_ppen_ed? Why are you looking for him?

He used to work at my club— he served drinks, dealt cards... stuff like that.

But I found out recently that he was also mixed up in some other stuff.

Mixed up in w_hat_? Can you please just tell me what the deal is?

It turns out he was dealing drugs for a guy named Rex Daniels.

And then three days ago, after a blowup between my guys and Rex's people, he told Rex he was done.

So? That's go_od_, right?

Yeah, except he owed Rex a lot of money.

Crud.

And he told Rex there was something he could give him that would more than pay off his debts.

But Rex said no, so Noah scooted out of there... but not before swiping Rex's ledger.

!

...which means now there are a lot of people out there looking for him who aren't exactly in a forgiving mood.

Because of the ledger?

Yeah—it has names, dates, drug-delivery amounts, you name it.

Crud.

Why are you so eager to find him?

Half Rex's guys had infiltrated my operation. If that ledger gets into the wrong hands, my operation goes down, too.

But I need help finding him. I don't even know his last name.

He's not here, is he?

No.

Noah's a good guy. Why can't everybody just leave him alone?

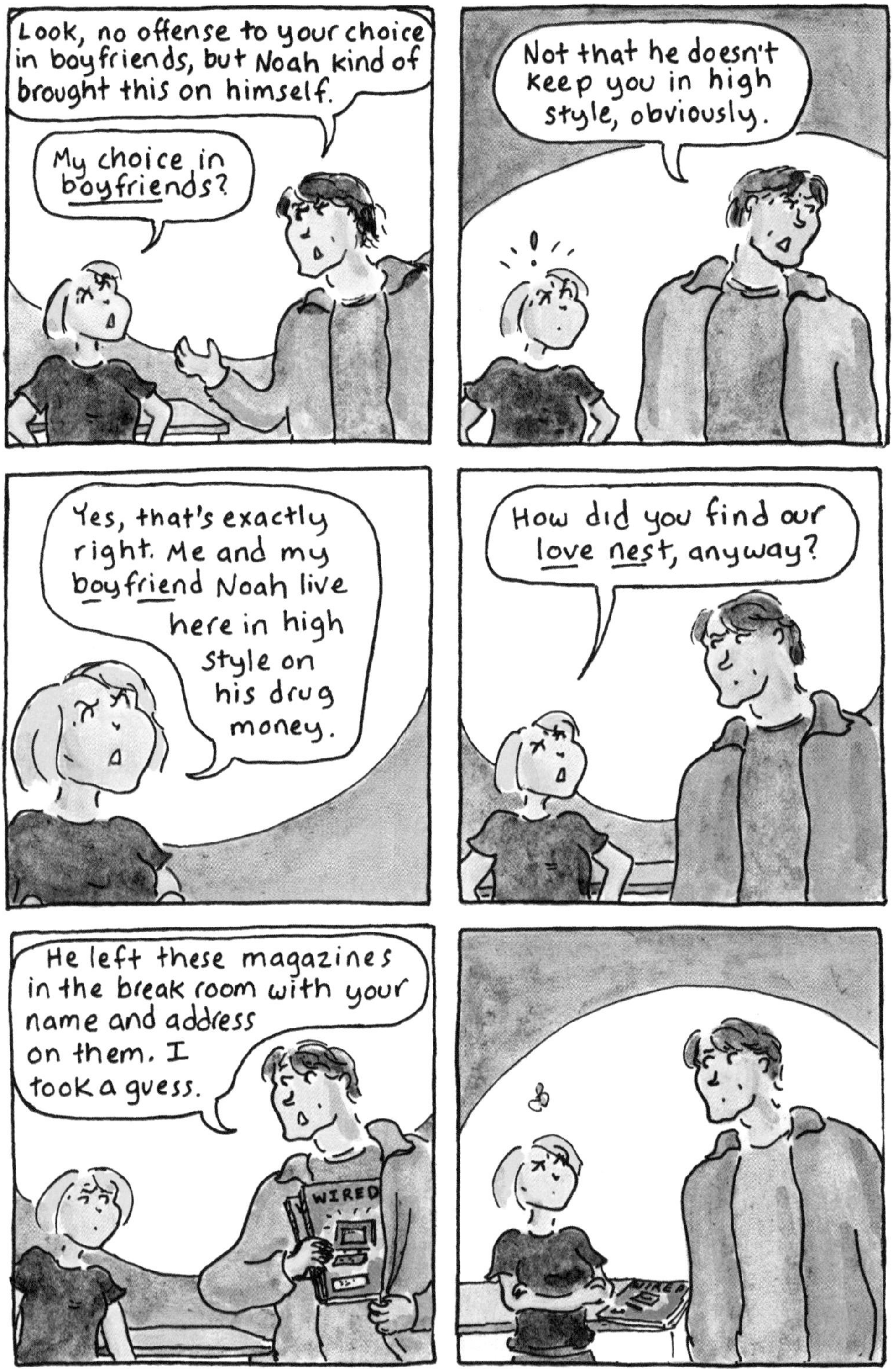
Look, no offense to your choice in boyfriends, but Noah kind of brought this on himself.
My choice in boyfriends?
Not that he doesn't keep you in high style, obviously.
!
Yes, that's exactly right. Me and my boyfriend Noah live here in high style on his drug money.
How did you find our love nest, anyway?
He left these magazines in the break room with your name and address on them. I took a guess.
WIRED
WIRED

Look, things will go much better for Noah if it's one of us who finds him rather than Rex's guys.

Is there anything you can tell me about where he might be?

No.

I think you should go.

OK. I understand.

So you have no thoughts on this at all?

37B

What was it Noah wanted to give Rex that would have paid off his debts?

A painting from the Norwood Museum.

?!

HOLY CRAP...

THE MINUTE GAMBLER GUY WAS GONE, I SCRAMBLED INTO MY STARLING DUDS.

MY HANDS WERE SHAKING, BUT THERE WAS NO PROCRASTINATION THIS TIME.

I TOOK OFF AT TOP SPEED TOWARD THE PLACE I'D BEEN AVOIDING FOR YEARS.

Amy! How nice of you to stop by!

I hope that's not something you wear to work, dear; it's a bit gaudy.

Where's Noah? Has he been here?

No, we haven't seen him since sometime last year, have we, honey?

No.

IF I WERE LOOKING FOR SOME-PLACE NO ONE WOULD EVER WANT TO FOLLOW ME, I'D COME HERE.

I CHECKED NOAH'S ROOM, BUT IT HAD CLEARLY BEEN CATS-ONLY FOR A WHILE NOW.

Are you staying for dinner?

Cat hair

I HAD AN OVERWHELMING DESIRE TO GET OUT OF THERE AS FAST AS POSSIBLE.

Not tonight.

If Noah does come by, or if you hear from him, can you let me know right away?

Of course, dear.

Bye, Dad.

Bye, Mom.

Bye, dea—

Oh! Does wittle whiskers need cuddle-wuddles?

...such the cutest wittle kitty-cat snookums...

I GOT AS FAR AS THE DERELICT BUS STOP ON THE CORNER BEFORE I THOROUGHLY LOST IT.

Amy?

Crud.

OF COURSE, THE ONE TIME I HADN'T PROCRASTINATED I'D BEEN FOLLOWED.

MY COVER WAS BLOWN BIG-TIME.

It's OK—I won't tell anyone.

Do you want a ride or anything?

I WAS MORTIFIED.

I'd prefer to have a nervous breakdown in private, if you don't mind.

Ok, sorry— I'll leave you alone.

If you want help finding him, though, call me.

Seriously— any-time— 24/7.

AS HE SPED OFF ON HIS MOTOR-CYCLE, I HAD THE URGE TO SUMMON HIM BACK, IF ONLY TO LET HIM KNOW THAT I DON'T USUALLY BLOW MY NOSE ON MY CAPE.

BACK HOME, THE WATER WORKS CONTINUED.

NOAH WAS SUCH A SWEET-NATURED GUY.

...AND MY BIGGEST FAN SINCE CHILDHOOD.

WAS I SUPPOSED TO BELIEVE HE WAS A DRUG-DEALING ART THIEF?

HIS DUFFEL BAG WAS STILL ON THE FLOOR.

I STARTED TEARING THROUGH IT, HOPING FOR SOME KIND OF CLUE.

IN A SIDE POCKET I FOUND A PHOTO.

XOXO-NIKKI

I STUCK IT IN MY WALLET.

AT THE BOTTOM OF THE BAG I FOUND A UNIFORM.

MY HEART SANK WHEN I SAW THE LABEL.

NOAH

NORWOOD MUSEUM

HANDS SHAKING, I DUG OUT THE E-READER SURVEY FORMS FROM THE MUSEUM GUARDS I'D TALKED TO.

Hi, Roger? Yes—it's Starling from the other night.

I PRETENDED TO BE FOLLOWING UP ON MY SURVEY.

...so you do think the buttons on an e-reader should ideally be large?

THEN I SEGUED CASUALLY TO OTHER MATTERS.

Hey, do you by any chance know a guard at the museum named Noah?

Noah Sturgess? Yeah, sure—he used to be on the Thursday shift with me.

Really? Do yo—

Someone said he called in yesterday, though, about taking a few weeks off.

Someone spoke to him just yesterday?

That's what they said.

SO AT LEAST HE'D BEEN ALIVE AND SPEAKING AS OF 24 HOURS AGO.

FOR NOW I'D HAVE TO TAKE COMFORT IN THAT.

AT WORK, THE DEADLINE FOR THE E-READER PRESENTATION WAS CLOSING IN.

WANTING TO KEEP THE DECKS CLEAR TO HELP NOAH, I DID PRECISELY WHAT I'D PROMISED MYSELF I WOULDN'T DO.

Hi, Claire?

Yeah, actually if you're still up for it, I'd love some help with those charts for the presentation.

Really? Thank you so much! You're a life-saver.

THERE WAS NO DENYING IT — SHE REALLY WAS.

PRESENTATION
Visuals ☑
Prototype ☑
Spiel ☐

OVER IN DINA'S OFFICE, THINGS WERE WINDING DOWN.

This place is going to be dusty by the time I get back from my honeymoon.

I'm jealous!

Yeah, but don't forget I still have 4 days of last-minute wedding planning to deal with.

Better than another week of Jason and the e-reader.

I'll give you that.

Just promise you won't let Jason mess you up.

If he's here and you're not when I get back, I'm going to be pissed.

I DUCKED OUT EARLY, HOPING TO GET A HANDLE ON THE NOAH SITUATION.

AT HOME, I FOUND WHAT LOOKED LIKE A REAL LETTER FOR ONCE IN MY MAILBOX.

IT WAS ONE OF MY E-READER FORMS, METICULOUSLY FILLED OUT.

E-reader Survey

CONTACT INFO:
Matt McRae
(555) 845-9866

IT MUST HAVE BEEN THE FORM I'D SHOVED AT HIM THE NIGHT OF THE FAKE BRAWL.

I DIALED THE NUMBER.

Hi, Matt? This is Amy Sturge-

Amy! Hang on...

THE BACKGROUND NOISE ON HIS END RECEDED.

What's going on? Is everything OK?

Yeah, I just had a question—

When Noah was working for you, do you remember a girl with purple spiked hair hanging around him— or maybe just coming to the club?

I think her name might be Nikki.

XOXO-Nikki

Not specifically. But there's a whole gang of punk kids who come over here sometimes from the Ulster Lounge. She could be one of those.

The Ulster Lounge? Ok - thanks.

Do you want me to go over there with you? They're kind of weird about who they let in.

No, I can handle it.

I do want to help, you know.

WHATEVER. I HUNG UP WITHOUT SAYING GOOD-BYE.

OUTSIDE THE ULSTER LOUNGE, A LONG LINE SNAKED AROUND THE CORNER.

UlsterLoun

AS I SHUFFLED TOWARD THE ENTRANCE, I RAN THE GIRL'S PHOTO BY MY NEIGHBORS IN LINE.

No—sorry. She doesn't look familiar.

THE BOUNCER WASN'T IMPRESSED BY MY ANN TAYLOR ENSEMBLE.

Sorry, Muffy—it's not prepster night.

But I just waited 45 minutes!

Tough. I'm going to have to ask you to step aside.

I just need to find someone.

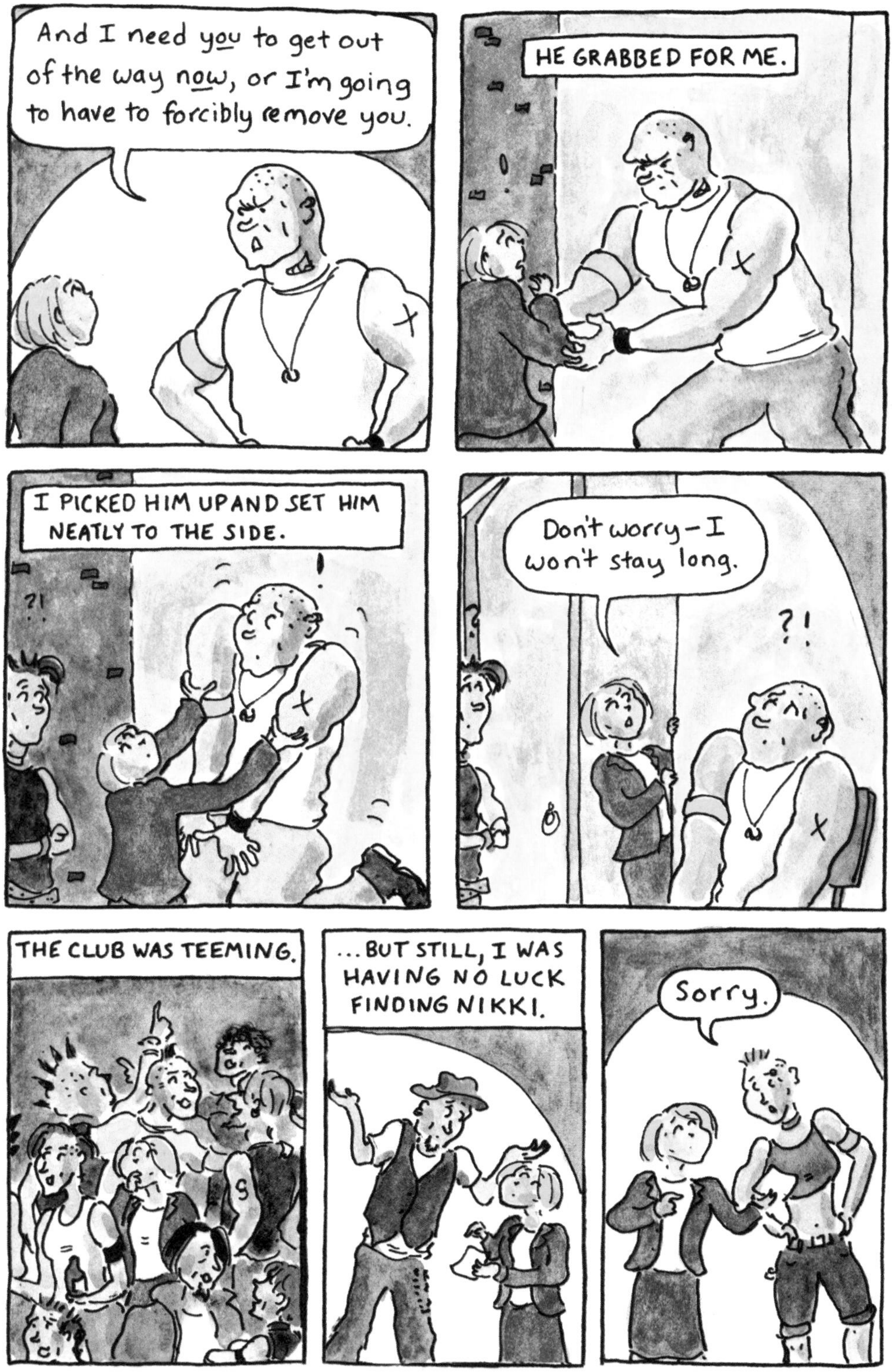
And I need you to get out of the way now, or I'm going to have to forcibly remove you.
HE GRABBED FOR ME.
I PICKED HIM UP AND SET HIM NEATLY TO THE SIDE.
!
?!
Don't worry – I won't stay long.
?!
THE CLUB WAS TEEMING.
...BUT STILL, I WAS HAVING NO LUCK FINDING NIKKI.
Sorry.

I WAS STARTING TO LOSE HOPE.

... UNTIL FINALLY I GOT A GLIMMER OF RECOGNITION.

Yeah, I've seen her. I think she's friends with the bartender.

BUT MY TIMING WAS OFF.

Sure, I know her to see her, but it's Luis she's friends with. He's off until Friday.

Crud. She was here last night, though. Luis gave her a bunch of bar food at the end of the night.

Does she usually get leftovers?

Not that I know of.

WAS SHE PUTTING NOAH UP SOMEWHERE? HE WAS CERTAINLY A BIG EATER.

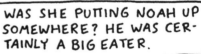

THE GUY GAVE ME LUIS'S NUMBER.

ON MY WAY HOME, I LEFT URGENT MESSAGE AFTER MESSAGE ON HIS VOICEMAIL.

Sorry to bother you again...

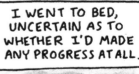

I WENT TO BED, UNCERTAIN AS TO WHETHER I'D MADE ANY PROGRESS AT ALL.

I WOULD HAVE COMPLETELY FORGOTTEN ABOUT MY TUESDAY MORNING "DATE" WITH RUSSELL IF HE HADN'T TEXTED.

Running late — see u in 10...

HE GREETED ME WITH A HUG.

Amy!

Hi, Russell.

IN MY HAZE OF STRESS, IT WAS SOOTHING TO HEAR ABOUT HIS NORMAL-PERSON PROBLEMS.

This pretrial hearing has been a complete disaster.

MY MIND WANDERED TO NOAH.

...which of course made me an hour late for my golf lesson.

AS WE PARTED WAYS, RUSSELL THANKED ME FOR MY ATTENTIVENESS.

You're a really good listener, you know that?

Claire would probably be complaining about not getting a word in edgewise!

A WAVE OF GUILT PASSED OVER ME.

Café

EVEN AS WE SPOKE, CLAIRE WAS BACK IN HER OFFICE, ASSEMBLING A SLEW OF CHARTS FOR MY PRESENTATION.

EVEN DAN WAS STARTING TO GET ANXIOUS AS D-DAY FOR THE SOLARIS MEETING APPROACHED.

So you've got everything under control?

TO BE HONEST, I HAD NO IDEA.

Mmm-hmm.

BUT THANKFULLY HE DIDN'T PRESS FOR SUPPORTING EVIDENCE.

Glad to hear it.

LATER HE CALLED ME INTO HIS OFFICE WITH JASON.

Amy— I know you have those ongoing irritable bowel issues.

...which is OK. But this is one meeting we really can't afford to botch.

...so can I ask you to make an extra copy of the e-reader presentation materials for Jason?

#!◎*?!!

And, Jason, if for any reason Amy can't be there, can you be prepared to fill in for her as master of ceremonies?

Happy to.

GREAT. ON TOP OF EVERYTHING ELSE, NOW I HAD TO WORRY THAT JASON WAS GOING TO POISON MY LUNCH OR SOMETHING.

ON MY WAY HOME, THE ULSTER LOUNGE BARTENDER FINALLY CALLED ME BACK.

Yeah, Nikki said she had friends coming over, so she wanted some extra food.

Really? Do you know where she lives?

Someplace called Sunrise House on the east side.

I LOOKED IT UP AND WENT OVER.

I'm looking for Nikki?

REFLECTIONS ON SOBER LIVING

Yeah, I'm Nikki's room-mate.

And is this guy also staying with you?

Does it look like we can fit another person in here?

Where's Nikki?

That's the 64,000-dollar question, isn't it?

I haven't seen her since Sunday.

Could you do me a huge favor and please call right away if she or this guy show up?

Yeah, ok—fine.

...But if it's smack you're looking for, you can get it a whole lot easier down on Adams Street.

SATURDAY MORNING, I GOT INTO MY BRIDESMAID GETUP AND CALLED A CAB.

Yes, 45 Baker Street.

ALMOST RIGHT AWAY THERE WAS A KNOCK AT THE DOOR.

I'm coming!... Geez, you guys are fast.

Amy—

What are you doing here?

I wanted to warn you- apparently Rex's guys found your address the same way I did, and they're sending people by to take you out.

Crud.

I'm leaving anyway; I'll be at a wedding all day.

But they'll be here when you get back, too. They think you might be hiding Noah.

Aw, man.

Is there someplace else you can stay for a while?

〈Sigh〉 Yeah— work, I guess.

But I don't have time to schlep my stuff over there — I'm already late.

Throw what you need into a bag.

I'll take it for now. You can come by the club after, and I'll drop you at work.

I DIDN'T HAVE TIME TO ARGUE. I GRABBED A HAPHAZARD ASSORTMENT OF CLOTHES AND MY E-READER STUFF AND SHOVED IT ALL INTO MY DUFFEL.

I HATED HANDING IT OFF.

I will take care of it.

THREE BLOCKS AWAY, I REALIZED I'D FORGOTTEN THE SILLY HAT THE BRIDESMAIDS WERE SUPPOSED TO WEAR.

Crud.

THE CABBIE WAITED WHILE I RAN BACK INSIDE.

BY THE TIME I CAME OUT, I'D PICKED UP NOT JUST THE HAT BUT—UNBEKNOWNST TO ME—A SMALL BAND OF STALKERS.

AT THE DAWSON ESTATE, THE BRIDESMAIDS WERE ALREADY GATHERING FOR THE PROCESSIONAL.

Thanks.

Is that your boyfriend?

Who?

The guy watching you with the binoculars.

He's cute.

?!

GREAT. DID I REALLY LOOK LIKE THE KIND OF PERSON WHO'D BRING HER BOYFRIEND TO A WEDDING IN A <u>HOODIE</u>?

HE AND HIS EQUALLY RATTY FRIEND SEEMED INTENT ON SNEAKING UP ON ME.

THEY COULD HAVE USED A FEW LESSONS IN SUBTLETY.

I PRETENDED NOT TO NOTICE.

BUT EVENTUALLY MR. HOODIE GOT SO CLOSE I COULD HEAR HIS NERVOUS BREATHING.

I WHIRLED AND SLAMMED HIM WITH A KNOCKOUT PUNCH.

...THEN I CHASED DOWN HIS COMPANION AND PUT HIM DECISIVELY OUT OF COMMISSION.

I HID BOTH OF THEM IN THE BUSHES, SO AS NOT TO SPOIL THE AMBIANCE FOR DINA'S GUESTS.

I SCANNED FOR FURTHER SIGNS OF TROUBLE.

BUT THE CEREMONY WAS AS LOVELY AND UNMARRED BY VIOLENCE AS DINA COULD HAVE HOPED.

AFTERWARDS, I ATE WITH MY FELLOW BRIDESMAIDS AND THEIR DATES.

THEN I SAT BACK AND WATCHED AS THE THRONGS HIT THE DANCE FLOOR.

UNCOMFORTABLY, I LET RUSSELL PULL ME, ALONG WITH CLAIRE, OUT ONTO THE FLOOR.

WE DANCED THROUGH ONE SONG...

... AND ANOTHER.

I WAS ABOUT READY TO SIT BACK DOWN WHEN CLAIRE LEANED IN.

I STARTED TO FOLLOW HER, BUT RUSSELL GRABBED MY HAND.

TO MY DISMAY, THE DJ OPTED JUST THEN FOR A SYRUPY BALLAD.

RUSSELL PULLED ME AGAINST HIM.

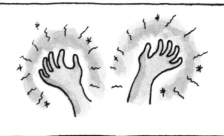

OH, CRUD. THAT WAS RIGHT. CAREFULLY I MOVED MY HANDS AWAY FROM HIS NECK.

I WAS FEELING A LITTLE SPARKING NOW.

BUT IT WAS MAINLY BECAUSE I WAS ON HIGH ALERT FOR MORE GOONS LIKE THE ONES WHO'D COME AFTER ME EARLIER.

I WAS TERRIFIED THAT CLAIRE WOULD COME BACK FROM THE BATHROOM AND FREAK OUT TO SEE US LIKE THIS.

I don't think lightning strikes for everyone.

I certainly hope not.

THE MOMENT THE SONG ENDED, I EXCUSED MYSELF.

I just need to get some air.

I BURROWED INTO THE CROWD BY THE DESSERT TABLE.

I'D DREAMED OF GETTING TOGETHER WITH RUSSELL.

BUT COULD I REALLY DO THAT TO CLAIRE?

SUDDENLY I SPOTTED A BIG GUY IN AN ILL-FITTING SUIT SHOULDERING HIS WAY TOWARD ME.

I STEELED MYSELF TO TAKE HIM ON.

...BUT BEFORE HE'D QUITE GOTTEN WITHIN STRIKING DISTANCE, A PAIR OF HANDS FROM UNDERNEATH THE TABLE GRABBED MY ANKLES AND THREW ME OFF BALANCE.

I CRASH-LANDED RIGHT ONTO THE DESSERTS.

DINA WAS NOT GOING TO BE PLEASED.

I ZAPPED THE JERK WHO'D PULLED ME DOWN.

THE MAN IN THE BAD SUIT WAS COMING UP FROM BEHIND.

I WHIRLED AND TOOK HIM OUT, TOO.

BUT I CAUGHT SIGHT OF YET AN-OTHER GUY, JUST AS HE STARTED TO LIFT DINA'S WEDDING CAKE.

DINA HAD DESIGNED THAT CAKE HERSELF.

I HURLED MYSELF AT THE GUY.

...AND SNAGGED THE CAKE JUST AS HE PREPARED TO LAUNCH IT.

HE SCAMPERED AWAY AS THE CROWD CLOSED IN AROUND ME.

Hold your horses, ma'am! Guests get cake after the bride and groom.

Did you see that bridesmaid?

She's totally trashed.

She was brawling with these frat guys by the desserts.

I SLUNK AWAY AND PRETENDED TO BE FASCINATED BY THE RARE SPECIMENS IN THE ESTATE'S ROSE GARDEN.

Amy?

RUSSELL HAD FOUND ME AGAIN.

Did you get some cake?

Oh—I see you did.

Frosting

They did have napkins next to the forks.

Yeah, well— my dress works, too, apparently.

You always were a strange bird, Amy.

HE LEANED IN AND KISSED ME.

I SHOULD HAVE STOPPED HIM, BUT I COULDN'T BRING MYSELF TO DO IT.

THANKFULLY MY FROSTING-
COVERED HANDS STAYED
BENIGNLY DORMANT THIS TIME.

You should find Claire.

I KNOW—
I need to sort things out with her.

No—wait...

I HAD A MILLION
CONFLICTING THOUGHTS.

Don't break up with Claire because of me.

I WASN'T SURE IF I MEANT
IT, OR IF I JUST DIDN'T WANT TO
PISS CLAIRE OFF BEFORE THE
E-READER PRESENTATION.

I shouldn't be going out with anyone until I get a bunch of things sorted out.

HE BLEW ME A KISS AND WENT
OUT THROUGH THE GATE.

I HAD NO IDEA WHAT HE
INTENDED TO DO.

I SAID MY FINAL CONGRATULATIONS TO DINA.

Well, you certainly look like you had a good time.

THEN I WENT TO WAIT FOR MY CAB AT THE END OF THE DRIVEWAY.

DAWSON ESTATE

LOST IN THOUGHT, I DIDN'T HEAR CAKE-THROWING MAN APPROACH.

DAWSON ESTATE

HE HIT ME SO ABRUPTLY FROM BEHIND THAT MY FOREHEAD SMACKED THE PAVEMENT.

BY THE TIME I'D SOMEWHAT GATHERED MY FACULTIES, HE'D DRAGGED ME HALFWAY TO HIS CAR.

HE SHOULD HAVE BEEN EASY FOR ME TO DEAL WITH, BUT MY HEAD WAS ACHING.

EVEN THE VOLTAGE IN MY HANDS SEEMED TO HAVE DIMMED.

WE WRESTLED FOR WHAT SEEMED LIKE HOURS, BUT WAS PROBABLY MORE LIKE TEN MINUTES.

BY THE TIME I'D FINALLY INCAPACITATED HIM, I WAS A MESS.

THE CABDRIVER INSISTED ON PUTTING DOWN A TOWEL BEFORE HE WOULD EVEN LET ME INTO THE CAR.

WHEN I GOT TO THE GAMBLING CLUB, THE PATRONS LOOKED AT ME LIKE SOME KIND OF RAVING LUNATIC IN OFF THE STREET.

I'm looking for Matt?

Uh, hang on.

Amy...

HE LOOKED HORRIFIED.

Come with me.

HE USHERED ME THROUGH A SIDE DOOR TO AN ELEVATOR.

Did you know you're bleeding?

Yeah—the cabdriver didn't really want me in his car.

You could have called me.

HE LED ME INTO AN APARTMENT.

IT WAS EVEN MORE BARE-BONES THAN MY OWN.

MY BAG WAS ON THE SOFA.

I can't just dump you off at your office like this.

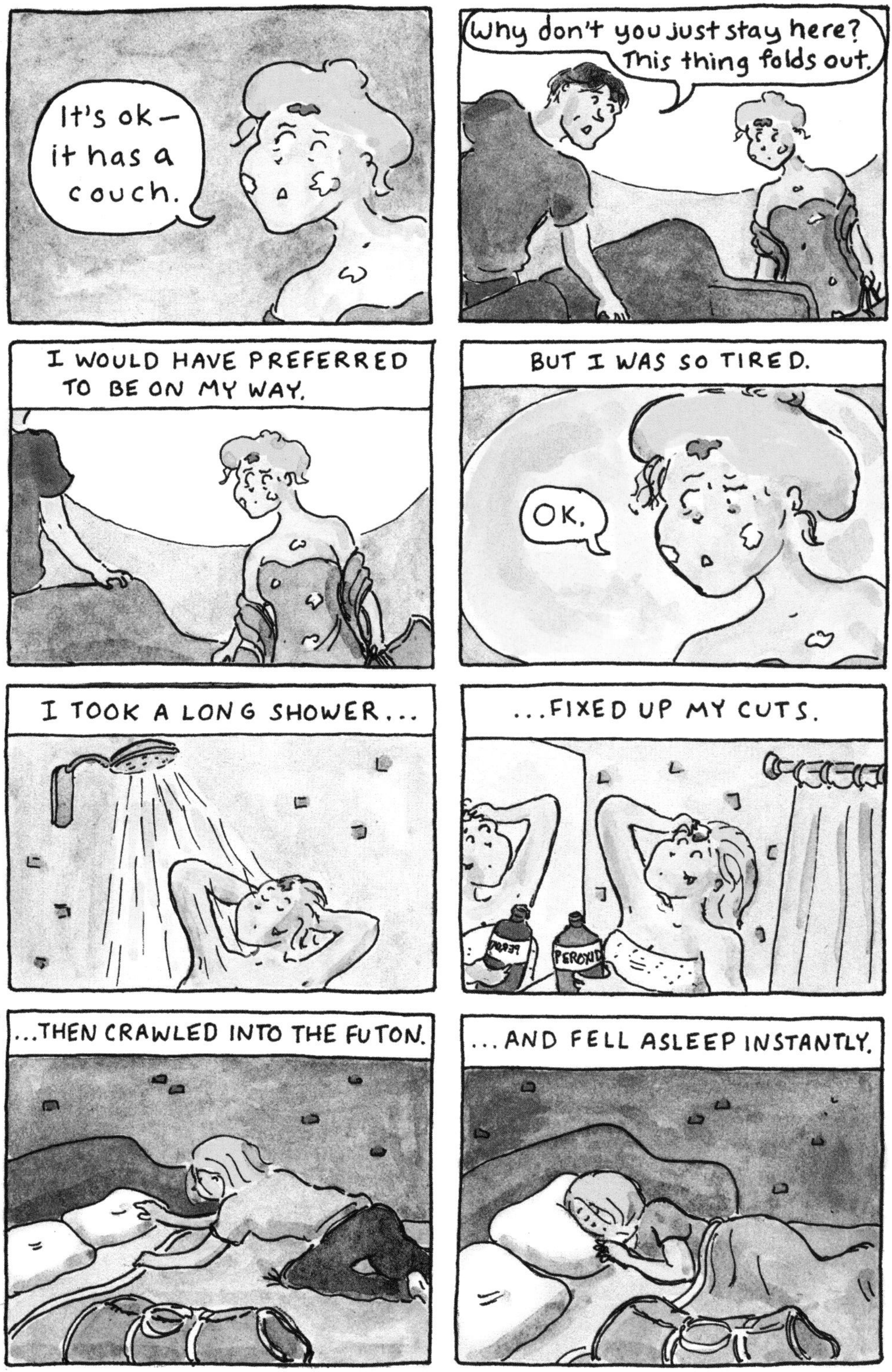
It's ok—
it has a couch.
Why don't you just stay here? This thing folds out.
I WOULD HAVE PREFERRED TO BE ON MY WAY.
BUT I WAS SO TIRED.
OK.
I TOOK A LONG SHOWER...
...FIXED UP MY CUTS.
PEROXID
...THEN CRAWLED INTO THE FUTON.
...AND FELL ASLEEP INSTANTLY.

WHEN I WOKE UP, IT WAS ALMOST 11.

MY HEAD WAS KILLING ME.

Hey, are you OK?

I'm fine.

What happened yesterday?

A bunch of goons followed me to the wedding.

I was off my game.

Do you know what they wanted?

Like you said— they probably think I know where Noah is.

Do you?

No.

My only lead is that girl Nikki I was telling you about.

I think she might be putting him up somewhere or feeding him or something.

Doesn't that bother you? Most girlfriends would flip out.

"Girlfriends"?

He's my brother.

That run-down house I followed you to the other day, with all the cats—what was that?

That's where my parents live. I thought maybe Noah would have gone home.

That's where you grew up?!

Yeah.

Wow.

And Noah and the rest of your family—do they have special abilities like you?

No, it's just that my mom happened to work in a chemical weapons factory while she was pregnant with me. I'm lucky I don't have three heads.

Geez.

You don't have to look at me like I'm pathetic. I can fly and beat people up.

That's not at all how I was looking at you.

I GOT DRESSED SO HE COULD DROP ME AT THE OFFICE.

You don't have to leave. I don't mind if you stay here.

That's OK — I have a bunch of work stuff to do anyway.

You can do it here. I have to go downstairs and deal with my own work stuff anyway.

At least you have food and a shower here.

SO I SPENT THE AFTERNOON ORGANIZING STUFF FOR THE E-READER CAMPAIGN.

WHEN MY ATTENTION SPAN FINALLY HIT A WALL, I GOT UP AND STRETCHED.

I COULDN'T RESIST A LITTLE SNOOPING.

PUNCHING BAG

That's the first fight I won.

I WAS MORTIFIED.

Sorry! I was being nosy.

That's ok. Those were my glory days.

Why'd you quit fighting?

I don't know—beating people up for money started to feel kind of lame after a while.

But why'd you go into the gambling business?

No special reason. The business was my trainer's. He left it to me when he moved to Florida.

So this was your locker? The one with Muhammad Ali?

Yeah, I always used to put pictures of my idols where I'd see them before my fights.

THE NEXT PICTURE STOPPED ME IN MY TRACKS.

HE TURNED BRIGHT RED.

Heh, yeah—I guess I didn't mention that you were one of them.

THIS TIME IT WAS ME WHO TURNED BRIGHT RED.

Matt...

ABRUPTLY MY PHONE RANG.

Amy! I need to talk to you.

IT WAS RUSSELL.

I told Claire.

You told Claire what?

I told her I wasn't sure about us. I didn't say it was because of you.

It shouldn't be because of me.

But after last night...

I told you — my life is really screwy right now. I shouldn't be—

But you told me before that you regretted bailing on things back when we were in college. Why not at least give it a chance this time?

HE HAD A POINT.

Can you meet me somewhere?

No, now's not good. If I want to have a prayer of keeping my job, I have to focus on that presentation.

Later in the week, then? Can we try a real date?

<Sigh> Yeah, ok— a real date later in the week.

Was that your boyfriend?

No... I don't know. Potentially...

MATT PICKED UP CHINESE FOOD FOR DINNER, AND WE WERE JUST SITTING DOWN TO EAT IT WHEN (RIGHT ON CUE) MY BUZZER WENT OFF.

Crud. Welcome to my world.

ALERT: Robbery in Progress: Lloyd's Jewels, C Street

You might as well start without me.

But your head— shouldn't you try not to reinjure it in case you have a concussion?

Yeah, well— crime never sleeps.

Save me a moo shi.

I SURPRISED THE THIEVES AS THEY WERE STUFFING THE LAST OF THE LOOT INTO THEIR BAGS.

I EFFICIENTLY ZAPPED ONE...

...THEN THE OTHER...

...AND WAS TYING THEM TO THE CASHIER'S DESK FOR THE POLICE WHEN A SHADOW FELL OVER ME.

Crud.

SO MUCH FOR AVOIDING JARRING HEAD MOVEMENTS. I PREPARED TO LAUNCH MYSELF AT THE GUY.

BUT ABRUPTLY...

CRASH

THE GUY TOPPLED SIDEWAYS.

Holy... Matt?!

What are you doing here? / I came on my bike.

I didn't think you should do this one by yourself.

I could have taken that guy. / I know.

But it wouldn't kill you to take it easy for a day or two. And anyway...

...that was pretty awesome.

I'm glad someone enjoys this stuff.

I TIED THE BIG GUY UP WITH THE OTHERS.

I brought you your moo shi.

I tried not to squish them too badly.

WE SAT BY THE CASH REGISTER AND MUNCHED CHINESE FOOD UNTIL THE POLICE CAME.

MONDAY, THE E-READER PROTO-
TYPE I'D SPECIAL-ORDERED FROM
THE MANUFACTURER ARRIVED.

AND CLAIRE CAME BY WITH THE
VISUALS FOR THE PRESENTATION.

Thank you so
much— these look
amazing.

CLAIRE HERSELF, ON THE OTHER
HAND, DIDN'T LOOK SO GOOD.

Sorry
I'm such
a mess.

Things with Russell sort of
fell apart over the weekend.

I'm sorry.

SORRIER THAN SHE KNEW...

Ugh—men! What are
you going to do?...

Anyway!
Good luck
tomorrow.

I'm keeping my
fingers crossed
for you.

I FELT LIKE PRETTY
MUCH THE BIGGEST
JERK EVER.

GRUDGINGLY I GAVE A COPY OF THE PRESENTATION MATERIALS TO JASON.

HE LOOKED ALL TOO HAPPY TO RECEIVE THEM.

I SAW HIM PRACTICING ALL AFTERNOON IN THE CONFERENCE ROOM.

I DUCKED OUT EARLY TO DO MY OWN PRACTICING AT MATT'S.

WITH MATT DOWNSTAIRS WORKING, I HAD THE WHOLE PLACE TO MYSELF.

I RAN THROUGH THE PRESENTATION MULTIPLE TIMES, WORKING OUT THE KINKS.

IN THE EARLY EVENING, MY PHONE RANG.

Call from:
Dr. Morris
Answer

I'D COMPLETELY FORGOTTEN MY AFTERNOON THERAPY APPOINTMENT.

But you're ok?

Yeah, I guess—considering.

I GOT HIM CAUGHT UP ON ALL THE LATEST.

Did you just say you have a date with Russell?

Yeah, I know—it's idiotic. Especially since it can't possibly even go anywhere.

It can't?

You know—because of that stupid thing with my hands.

Russell's the only person I've ever even kissed.

...and it only worked this time because I was so distracted. If I'd actually gotten carried away, I'd probably have accidentally electrocuted him again.

OK, but don't you think—

SUDDENLY I REALIZED MATT WAS STANDING THERE.

I have to go!

PEPPERONI

I WAS HORRIFIED. HOW LONG HAD HE BEEN LISTENING?

PEPPERONI

I WAS TOO EMBARRASSED TO ASK.

I brought pizza.

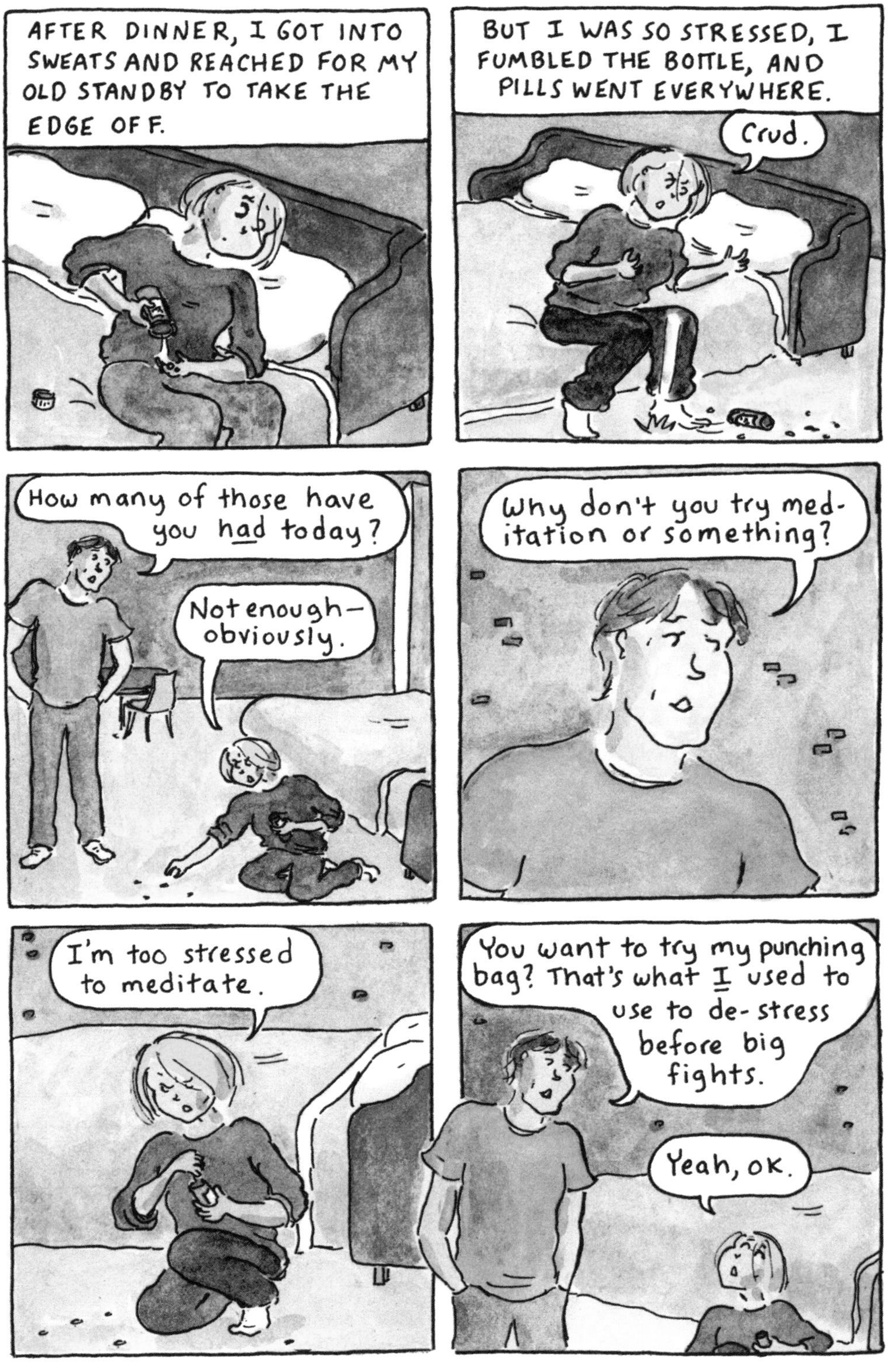
AFTER DINNER, I GOT INTO SWEATS AND REACHED FOR MY OLD STANDBY TO TAKE THE EDGE OFF.
BUT I WAS SO STRESSED, I FUMBLED THE BOTTLE, AND PILLS WENT EVERYWHERE.
Crud.
How many of those have you had today?
Not enough—obviously.
Why don't you try meditation or something?
I'm too stressed to meditate.
You want to try my punching bag? That's what I used to use to de-stress before big fights.
Yeah, ok.

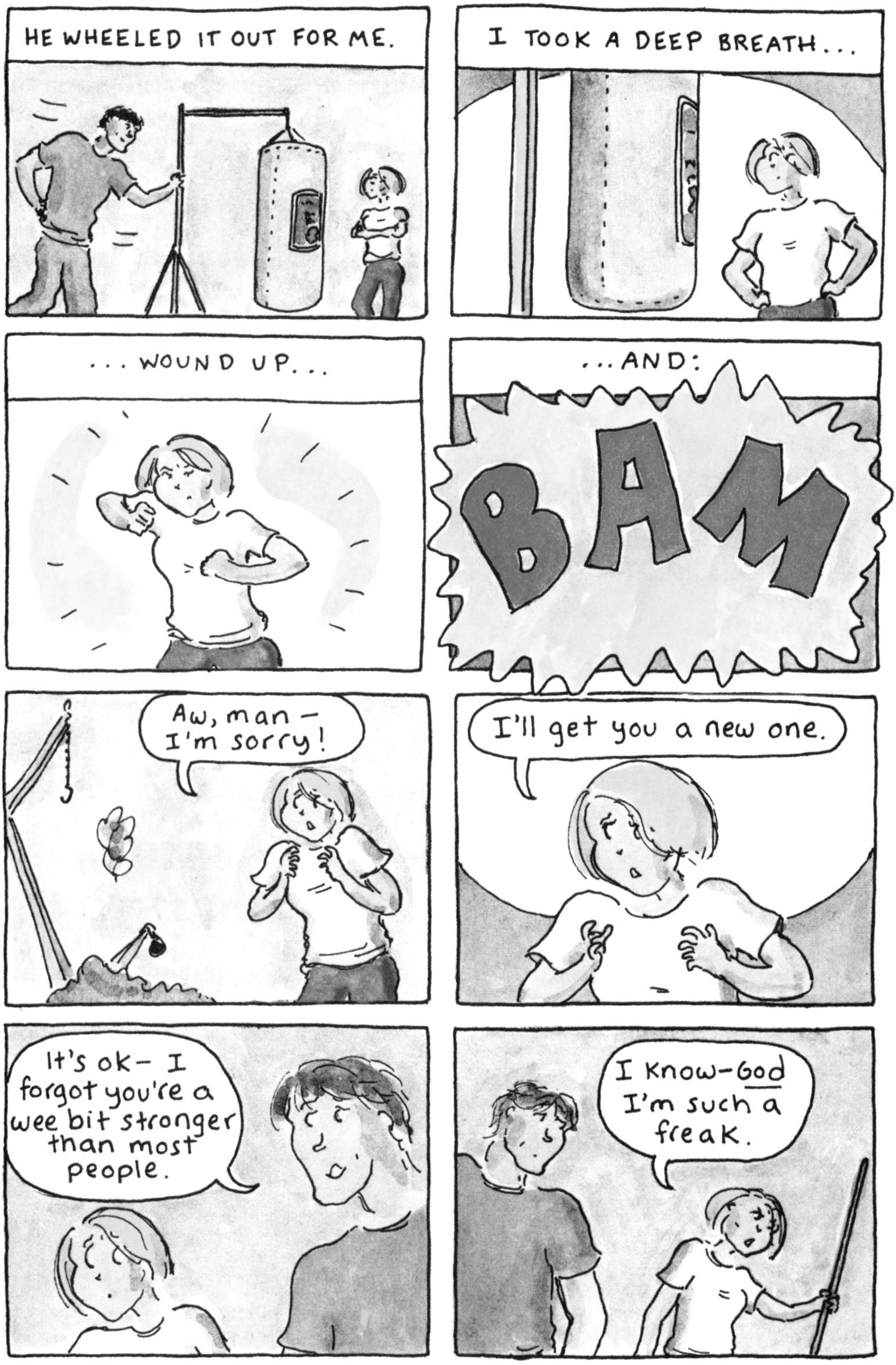
HE WHEELED IT OUT FOR ME.
I TOOK A DEEP BREATH...
...WOUND UP...
...AND:
BAM
Aw, man — I'm sorry!
I'll get you a new one.
It's ok— I forgot you're a wee bit stronger than most people.
I know—God I'm such a freak.

HE KEPT UP THE SHOULDER RUB EVEN AS I STARTED TO GET SLEEPY.

JUST AS I STARTED TO DRIFT OFF, I FELT HIS HAND BRUSH MY CHEEK, AND I OPENED MY EYES.

I HOPED HE DIDN'T NOTICE THAT A SMALL SHOWER OF SPARKS FLEW OUT FROM MY HAND.

IN THE MORNING, I PUT ON MY MOST WRINKLE-FREE SUIT.	... AND TUCKED THE E-READER PROTOTYPE INTO MY POCKET.

Today's D-day, huh?

Yeah.

The meeting's not until 11:30, but I'm planning to camp out in the conference room so this creep Jason doesn't bump me from my own presentation.

Good plan.

I CLEARED AWAY MY BREAK-FAST OF CHAMPIONS.

THEN I HEADED OUT, MENTALLY REVIEWING THE HIGHLIGHTS OF MY PRESENTATION AS I WENT.

I WAS BARELY TO THE END OF THE STREET WHEN MY PHONE RANG.

Hey, this is Cheryl—Nikki's roommate? You said to call if she showed up.

What—is she there?

She was. She came and grabbed some clothes.

She just left, like two minutes ago.

Did she say where she was going?

No. She never tells me anything.

Crud.

SUNRISE HOUSE WASN'T THAT FAR AWAY.

I TOOK OFF AT A SPRINT.

Whoa! Windy today!

WAY DOWN ON C STREET, I CAUGHT SIGHT OF A SMALL PURPLE-HAIRED FIGURE, LADEN WITH BAGS.

ONE OF THEM LOOKED LIKE NOAH'S DUFFEL.

...WHICH MEANT SHE'D BEEN TO THE APARTMENT.

I FOLLOWED AT A DISTANCE.

AT CITY CENTER SHE HOPPED ON THE 138 BUS.

I GOT ON BEHIND HER.

I GOT A SINKING FEELING AS THE NEIGHBORHOODS GOT MORE AND MORE FAMILIAR.

SURE ENOUGH, WHEN THE DRIVER CALLED THE TYLER STREET STOP, SHE STOOD UP.

I FOLLOWED HER OUT AND WATCHED IN DISMAY AS SHE HEADED DOWN THE STREET TOWARD THE HOUSE OF HAIR BALLS.

BYPASSING THE FRONT WALK, SHE DARTED AROUND BACK.

I FUMBLED IN MY BRIEFCASE FOR MY PILLS.

JUST THEN, A CAR CAME SCREECHING UP TO THE CURB.

That way!

CRUD. I WASN'T THE ONLY ONE TAILING NIKKI.

SHE MUST HAVE PICKED UP REX'S GOONS ALONG WITH NOAH'S BAG AT THE APARTMENT.

I GULPED MY PILLS...

...AND RACED AFTER EVERYONE.

IN THE DIM LIGHT I SAW AN IMPROVISED SLEEPING AREA.

HAD NOAH BEEN HERE ALL ALONG?

I HEARD SCUFFLING NOISES AND THUMPS, AND MADE MY WAY DEEPER INTO THE CELLAR.

THE DOOR TO THE UP-STAIRS WAS AJAR.

I TOOK THE STAIRS TWO AT A TIME.

Amy! You, too?!

What has gotten into you kids? We don't see you for ages, and then you both show up with a gang of rowdy friends?

"Noah's here?" "Yes. I don't know what game they're playing, but he and his friends just went stampeding upstairs."

I BOUNDED UP AFTER THEM.
"I think it was 'kill the Carrier.'"

THE ACTION SEEMED TO BE IN NOAH'S ROOM.

"I said, where is it?" "I told you, I don't—"

SMACK

"Leave him alone!" "Who the...?"

"Oh, right—it's the bridesmaid from Hell."

I CROUCHED TO LUNGE AT HIM.

"Sorry, sweetheart..."

"I'm afraid your fancy jujitsu moves aren't going to work so well on this."

CRUD. HE WAS RIGHT. I MIGHT BE FAST AND STRONG, BUT I WASN'T BULLETPROOF.

AND THAT WAS A NASTY-LOOKING WEAPON.

P.J.! Take her briefcase.

THE BALD GUY YANKED MY BRIEFCASE AWAY.

... THEN DUMPED ITS CONTENTS ON THE FLOOR.

... AND STARTED RIFFLING HAPHAZARDLY THROUGH MY CAREFULLY ORGANIZED PRESENTATION MATERIALS.

It's just a bunch of charts.

Keep them. We don't know what they're for.

THE GUY STARTED SHOVING THE PAPERS INTO HIS PANTS.

No!...

I need that stuff for work!

Oh, yeah? Well — your friend here has an important notebook that we kind of need for work. So I think we're even.

IF THESE GUYS DIDN'T KILL NOAH, I WAS ABOUT READY TO DO IT MYSELF.

Where the h<u>e</u>ll is the ledger?

The cat box... At the bottom of the stairs. Under the kitty litter.

P.J.— g<u>o</u>!

MY MOM'S PIERCING VOICE CARRIED UP FROM DOWNSTAIRS.

Young man! This is for the cats! We have a per- fectly good bathroom upstairs!

HE RETURNED WITH A PLASTIC BAG.

THE CATS HAD SCRATCHED HOLES IN IT, AND THE NOTEBOOK INSIDE WAS A GLUEY PULP, REEKING OF CAT PEE.

You let this happen to Rex Daniels's operations manual? What did you think was going to hap- pen to y<u>ou</u>?

Aagh

I COULDN'T JUST STAND THERE AND WATCH MY LITTLE BROTHER GET PUMMELLED.

I LAUNCHED MY-
SELF AT THE GUY.

HE WHIRLED
TOWARD ME.

IT WAS LIKE
SLOW MOTION.

HE AIMED THE GUN
STRAIGHT AT ME.

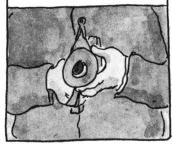

. . . AND FIRED.

THE BULLET
SAILED
TOWARD ME.

. . . TOO FAST FOR
ME TO DODGE.

IT WENT STRAIGHT
INTO MY CHEST.

NOAH SHOUTED
AS I STAGGERED
BACKWARDS. . .

NOOOOOOO

. . . AND COLLAPSED.

. . . DEAD.

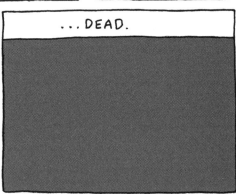

...OR AT LEAST I WAS PRETTY SURE I WAS DEAD.

...EXCEPT... I COULD STILL HEAR TALKING.

Holy... You effing killed her!

AND THEN MY MOM:

That's enough rough-housing! It's 10:45. I'm taking your father to his allergy appointment. I expect to see you kids outside when we get back!

HER FOOTSTEPS RETREATED.

What a nutjob.

SUDDENLY HER WORDS SANK IN: 10:45?! MY PRESENTATION WAS AT 11:30...

!

FORGETTING I WAS DEAD, I BOLTED UPRIGHT.

I have to get out of here!

NOAH FAINTED, NIKKI SHRIEKED, AND MY MURDERER AND HIS CRONIES STUMBLED BACKWARDS.

AAAGH!

?

What the hell?!

I told you at the wedding: she's some kind of undead thing!

Please! Leave us alone!

We'll do whatever you say!

Oh, give it a rest. You just *shot* me.

I ZAPPED TWO OF THEM.

Z†††††

THE OTHER GUY STILL HAD MY PRESENTATION IN HIS PANTS.

I need my stuff.

TO HIS CREDIT, HE DID TRY.

BUT HE WAS SHAKING SO BADLY, AND HIS PANTS HAD SO MANY BUTTONS, HE COULDN'T GET THEM UNDONE.

Oh, forget it. I'll get the stuff out later.

ZAP

NIKKI WAS BENT OVER NOAH.

He's bleed-ing.

I know—we need to call an ambulance.

But I need you to help me with one thing first.

Where's the Norwood Museum painting?

SHE FLINCHED.

I don't know what—

Nikki. I _know_ about the painting.

If that thing turns up here, Noah could go to jail for the rest of his life.

...Or I can return it, and we can all pretend this never happened.

I FOLLOWED HER DOWN TO THE BASEMENT.

SHE PULLED A WRAPPED PACKAGE FROM UNDER NOAH'S MATTRESS.

I WANTED TO UNWRAP IT AND TAKE A LOOK.

BUT IT WAS GETTING LATE.

I CALLED AN AMBULANCE FOR NOAH.

...That's right— 26 Tyler Street.

THEN I HESITATED.

I WAS ITCHING TO JET TO THE OFFICE IN MY USUAL SELF-PROPELLED WAY.

BUT MY PRESENTATION WAS STILL STUCK IN THE GUY'S PANTS.

...AND I HAD TWO OTHER GOONS TO DISPOSE OF BEFORE MY PARENTS GOT BACK.

IT WAS DOUBTFUL I COULD BALANCE THREE GUYS AND FLY AT THE SAME TIME WHILE CARRYING MY GOOD WORK SUIT.

RELUCTANTLY I MADE ANOTHER CALL.

Amy! How's it going?

Fine.

Really? You sound kind of—

OK—not fine. Do you think you could give me a ride from my parents' house?

From your—?

Sure thing—I'll be right there.

I COULD HEAR THE AMBU-
LANCE APPROACHING.

Do you want to go to the hospital with Noah?

Yes.

Ok, so, uh, I don't know what kind of messed-up stuff Noah's into...

So if the medics ask, can you just say he got jumped by some punks in the neighborhood or some-thing?

WARINESS OF AUTHORITY DIDN'T SEEM LIKE SUCH A HARD SELL FOR THIS GIRL.

Ok.

JUST AFTER THE AMBULANCE LEFT, MATT PULLED UP TO THE CURB.

Where to? Your office?

?

Yeah, but I have to get rid of these guys first.

Robbins Park?

That works.

I BALANCED THE GUYS ON MY LAP.

AT THE PARK, I PROPPED THEM ON AN EMPTY BENCH.

What about this guy?

<sigh>

?

My whole presentation is in his pants.

But I don't have time to deal with it now; I need to get to the office.

OK. Hang on.

HE REVVED THE ENGINE, AND WE WERE OFF.

BUT NO SOONER HAD WE MADE IT ONTO THE EXPRESSWAY THAN A POLICE CRUISER PULLED IN BEHIND US, LIGHTS FLASHING.

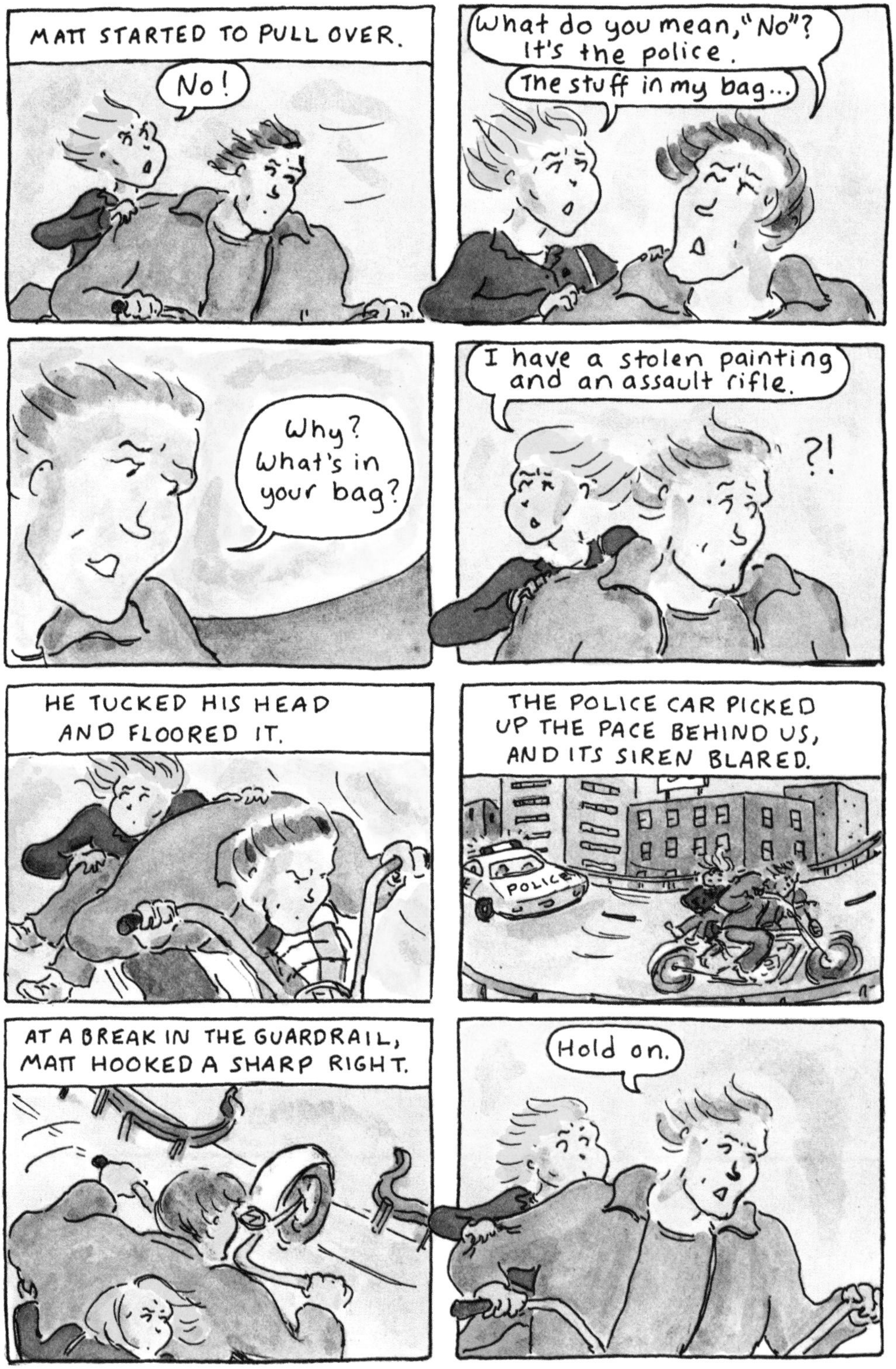
MATT STARTED TO PULL OVER.
No!
What do you mean, "No"? It's the police.
The stuff in my bag...
Why? What's in your bag?
I have a stolen painting and an assault rifle.
?!
HE TUCKED HIS HEAD AND FLOORED IT.
THE POLICE CAR PICKED UP THE PACE BEHIND US, AND ITS SIREN BLARED.
POLICE
AT A BREAK IN THE GUARDRAIL, MATT HOOKED A SHARP RIGHT.
Hold on.

THE BIKE SAILED OFF
THE EXPRESSWAY...

... OVER EVERETT STREET...

...AND INTO THE ALLEY BETWEEN
TWO APARTMENT BUILDINGS.

Oof!

THUNK

WE DARTED THE REST OF THE
WAY THROUGH BACKSTREETS.

... CAREENING PAST PARKED CARS...

...AND STARTLED PEDESTRIANS.

Sorry!

AS HE SCREECHED UP TO THE
FRONT OF MY BUILDING, I
JUMPED OFF THE BIKE.

Thank you.

I RACED UPSTAIRS.

JASON WAS ALREADY IN THE CONFERENCE ROOM, HOLDING FORTH.

CLASSIC JASON—HE'D ACTUALLY LOCKED THE DOOR TO KEEP ME OUT.

I APPLIED SOME CONTROLLED PRESSURE AND SNAPPED THROUGH THE BOLT.

THE DOOR SWUNG OPEN WITH A SHARP CRACKING NOISE.

JASON WAS STARTLED.

Amy! Good of you to drop by.

We're pretty much all set here at this point. So if you've got other work to do, I'll just go ahead and finish up with our clients.

That's ok. I can take it from here.

Amy, your assistance on this project has been invaluable, but I think it's better if we don't confuse matters for our clients by switching gears half-way through.

My assis-tance?

ONE OF THE SOLARIS GUYS CHUCKLED SYMPATHETICALLY.

My assistant's the same way: she gets pretty proprietary about projects after I've had her do the back-end research.

Ok, but in this case, this is actually my accou—

JASON PUT A HAND ON MY SHOULDER.

Amy—we can talk about this later. But for now I think I should really get back to where we were be-fore you interrupted.

I WAS APOPLECTIC.

BUT A MESSY SCENE IN THE MIDST OF OUR PITCH MEETING COULD TORPEDO EVERYTHING I'D WORKED FOR.

I SAT DOWN, SEETHING.

Getting back to my question— the focus group data you reference seems a bit unorthodox; there's a lot of input from law enforcement, victims of crime, people in non-white-collar careers...

...Isn't that not really the target market we're looking for, considering the kind of high-end product we have in mind?

Actually, it's—

BUT JASON PLOWED RIGHT OVER ME.

That shouldn't be a problem...

As I recall, it's simply a reflection of the fact that Amy wasn't able to follow through with a focus group she had planned with the kinds of affluent customers you had in mind.

But I'd be happy to follow up with that myself as I move forward with the project.

That would be great. Thanks so much, Jason.

Can I have my assistant call you next week to schedule a follow-up discussion?

Absolutely. Here's my card.

And is this number direct, or does it go to Amy, your secretar—

I AM NOT JASON'S SECRETARY!!!

OOPS...

SO MUCH FOR AVOIDING A SCENE.

BUT NOW THAT THAT SHIP HAD SAILED...

In fact...

...I COULDN'T HOLD BACK NOW.

Jason has had no involvement in this project whatsoever.

...until today, when he was brought in to serve as last-minute backup because I was detained on my way here.

...which, I might add, goes some way to explaining why he so thoroughly fails to grasp the fundamental selling points of the product.

IT WAS JASON WHO BROKE THE DISCONCERTED SILENCE THAT FOLLOWED.

Heh, I'm afraid you'll have to excuse her, folks...

...as is regrettably obvious, Amy's been suffering from some mental health issues lately.

You cannot be seri—

BUT THE SOLARIS GUY WAS TOTALLY FOCUSED ON THE PRODUCT.

These selling points you mention... what specifically are you referring to?

I WAS GRATEFUL TO BE BACK ON TOPIC.

OK, for example, you asked about our focus group demographics, which, as you say, are a bit unorthodox.

That's because this is an untapped sector.

Your competitors who got into the field a long time ago already have the upscale market covered.

...But security, law enforcement, blue collar... people like struggling musicians living in sketchy neighborhoods...

If you identify those people's needs and tailor a product to them, you'll have an entire market segment to yourself.

And would it really be feasible to deliver the product at a price point these people can afford?

Didn't Jason show you the data models?

Of course I did.

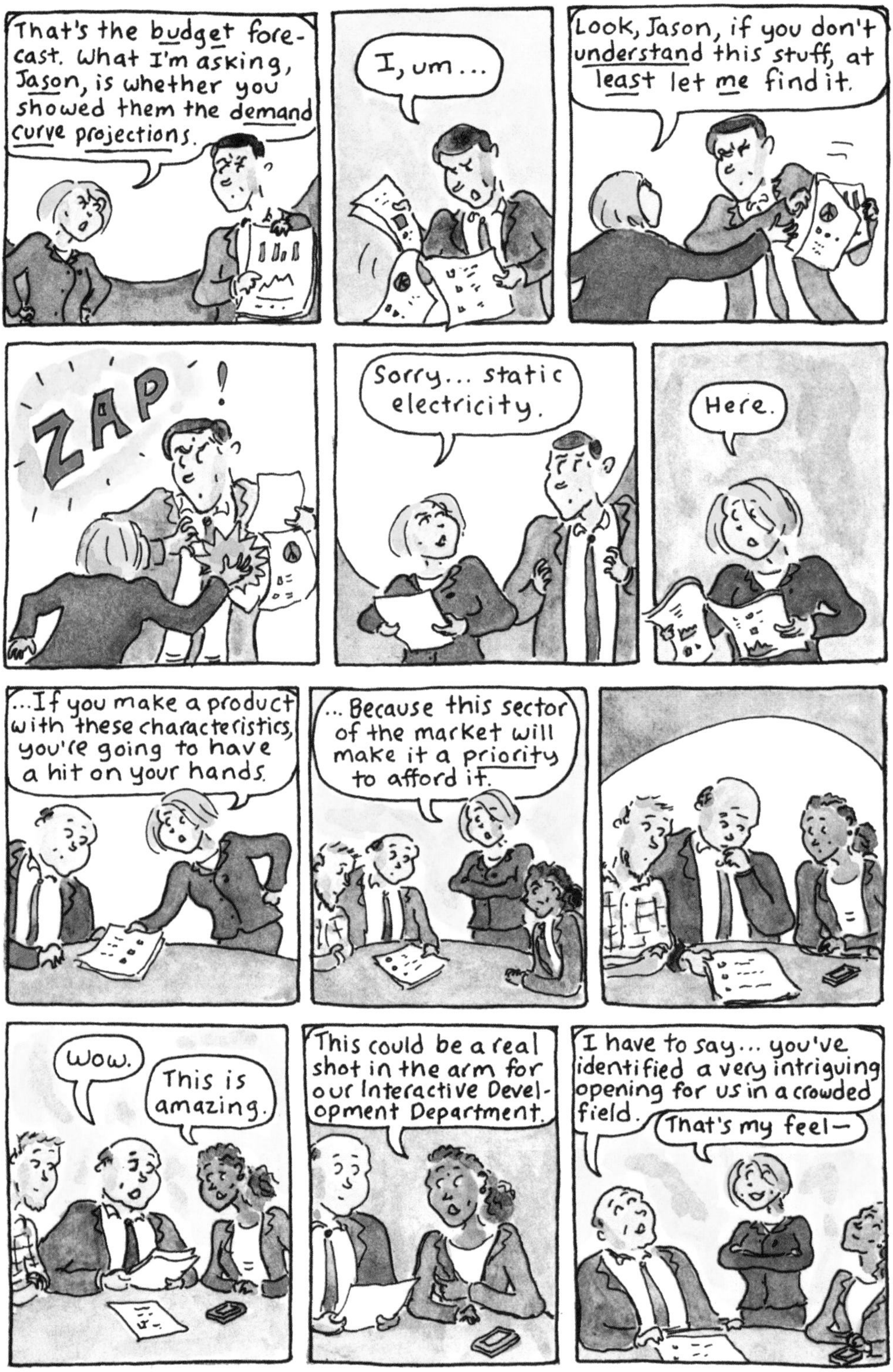
That's the budget forecast. What I'm asking, Jason, is whether you showed them the demand curve projections.
I, um...
Look, Jason, if you don't understand this stuff, at least let me find it.
ZAP!
Sorry... static electricity.
Here.
...If you make a product with these characteristics, you're going to have a hit on your hands.
...Because this sector of the market will make it a priority to afford it.
Wow.
This is amazing.
This could be a real shot in the arm for our Interactive Development Department.
I have to say... you've identified a very intriguing opening for us in a crowded field.
That's my feel—

Amy?!

?

MATT WAS STANDING IN THE DOORWAY.

HE WAS LOOKING WINDED AND DISHEVELED.

I'm sorry to interrupt... You left your materials in—

Matt McRae?!

Yes.

It's an honor to meet you! I'm a huge UFC fan.

Thank you.

I didn't mean to break up the meeting. I just wanted to get these papers to—

I'm sorry—could I trouble you for a photo?

Um, sure—ok.

Wait—this is amazing. Are you here as a potential spokesperson for the e-reader?

HE LOOKED AT ME UNCERTAINLY.

Uh, possibly...

HE'D CLEARLY BEEN PAYING ATTENTION TO THE SPIEL I'D BEEN PRACTICING IN HIS APARTMENT.

Amy's been really convincing about how this reader is different from the typical yuppie gadget you might expect.

I saw the prototype she designed, too, and it's really impressive—like something you could get military contracts with—or law enforcement.

Oh, and, uh— Amy, I don't know if you still need these notes, but you had accidentally left them downstairs.

Typical.

Pardon?

Oh, nothing...

...Just typical Amy... waltzing in here fifteen minutes late—without her notes—expecting everyone to just excuse her unprofessionalism.

You do know the reason Amy was late today is because she was attacked on her way here.

Oh my God—are you OK?

I'm alright.

You didn't say anything.

I didn't want to detract from the focus of the—

Holy—is that a bullet hole?

That's, like, a shotgun-blast hole. How are you even here?

I don't know.

I REALLY DIDN'T.

I'D BEEN SHOT IN THE LEG ONCE BY A MUCH LESSER GUN DURING MY EARLY YEARS AS STARLING...

...AND WHILE NOT AS DIRE AS IT WOULD HAVE BEEN FOR A NORMAL PERSON, THE WOUND HAD HARDLY BEEN INSIGNIFICANT.

MATT HURRIED OVER.

Does it hurt?

Yeah, but just kind of like a bad bruise.

I WAS AFRAID TO LOOK. BUT IT SEEMED CLEAR MATT WASN'T GOING ANY- WHERE UNTIL I DID.

GINGERLY, I PEEKED UNDER MY BLAZER.

?!

?

Hey, what do you know? The proto- type I made really is bulletproof.

My God—that thing saved your life!

Looks like it still works, too!

Not a bad selling point— "This reader could save your life"!

Claire Hayes over at Wallensby Advertising is really good. I bet she could come up with something really punchy to promote that concept.

The print mock-ups Jason showed us earlier were good. Who did those?

I, um— I'm not 100% sure offhand, but I'd be happy to—

Those were Claire's. She's good, isn't she?

She is. Can we set up a meeting with her?

Sure—I can put you in touch tomorrow.

And, Matt—are you in fact on board with the idea of a product endorsement, assuming we can work out the details?

If Amy's point person on the account, I'd be happy to do it.

Of course.

You know...

...someone else I have a passing acquaintance with is Starling.

?

Really?!

Yes, it occurs to me there's a chance she might be willing to do an endorsement for this, too... if the price were right.

That's genius! A joint Starling-Matt McRae campaign is an amazing idea!

I'll see what I can do...

BY THE TIME THE MEETING BROKE UP, I HAD A STACK OF BUSINESS CARDS AND A LONG LIST OF FOLLOW-UP ITEMS TO LOOK INTO.

OK, great—we'll talk to you tomorrow.

Thanks so much.

JASON LOOKED LIKE HE WOULDN'T MIND TAKING A SHOTGUN BLAST AT ME HIMSELF.

MATT FOLLOWED ME TO MY DESK.

You were awesome in there!

Thanks.

But, geez— that was a close call this morning.

I know—I can't believe I almost let Jason steal that account right out from under me.

No, I mean before that— you could have been killed.

I SHUDDERED.

Yeah, that...

I wish you'd called me before you went in after those guys.

Yeah, I know... I just—

BUT HE WAS GONE

?

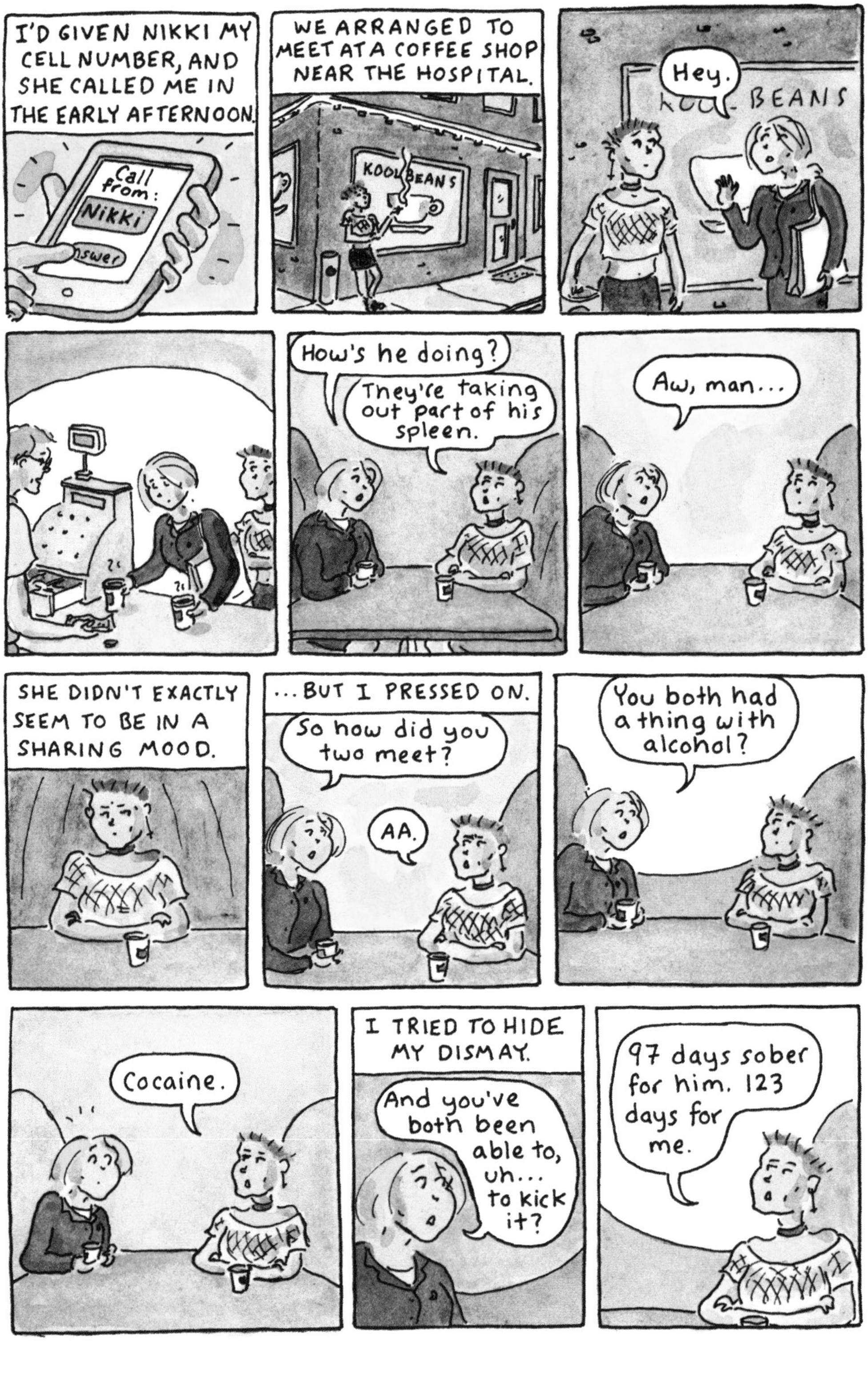
I'D GIVEN NIKKI MY CELL NUMBER, AND SHE CALLED ME IN THE EARLY AFTERNOON.
Call from:
Nikki
WE ARRANGED TO MEET AT A COFFEE SHOP NEAR THE HOSPITAL.
KOOL BEANS
Hey.
BEANS
How's he doing?
They're taking out part of his spleen.
Aw, man...
SHE DIDN'T EXACTLY SEEM TO BE IN A SHARING MOOD.
...BUT I PRESSED ON.
So how did you two meet?
AA.
You both had a thing with alcohol?
Cocaine.
I TRIED TO HIDE MY DISMAY.
And you've both been able to, uh... to kick it?
97 days sober for him. 123 days for me.

That's great.

So how'd he get into this mess with Rex Daniels's people?

You know— usual story...

He was making decent money selling for Rex out of Fight Club wagerers. Then he got hooked and started snorting up the merchandise himself.

And that's what got him into debt?

Big-time.

15,000 dollars.

Ok, I kind of get how that happens.

...but a major art heist?? What was he thinking?!

FOR THE FIRST TIME SHE LOOKED RUFFLED.

I have no effing clue.

And it sounds like it didn't do him any good anyway?

No.

It would have paid off way more than Noah owed. But Rex wouldn't take it.

Why not?

He said having to unload a high-profile painting wasn't worth the risk.

I KIND OF HAD TO AGREE WITH HIM THERE.

So then what? Noah just ran off with Rex's ledger?

The guy who runs Fight Club Wagerers caught people dealing and figured out Rex had turned it into a major distribution point.

...So he started getting all hard-ass about it, and there was this big brawl, and in the middle of it Rex's enforcer threatened Noah with a gun because he still hadn't paid off his debts.

THAT PART SOUNDED ALL TOO FAMILIAR.

And then Noah said you found out he was mixed up in this stuff and made him promise to stop.

GREAT. IT WAS SOUNDING LIKE THIS WAS SHAPING UP TO BE ALL MY FAULT.

I didn't tell him to antagonize the organization— I just told him to get away from those guys.

Well, Rex wasn't about to let Noah just walk away while he was still on the hook for all that money.

And Noah figured if Rex's organization was on the ropes anyway—since it was losing Fight Club—he'd just try to help it along.

What, so he thought he could just take the whole thing down by stealing the ledger?

I don't know. Rex thought Noah was coming by to pay him, but instead Noah pilfered the notebook and went into hiding.

Great. So now what? Is he planning to hide for the rest of his life?

<Sigh> I don't know.

I never said he's not an idiot.

What a mess.

He's lucky you stick around to keep an eye on him.

Yeah, well — lucky for him, he's kind of an endearing idiot.

SHE PROMISED TO LET ME KNOW HOW HE WAS DOING.

FROM THE COFFEE SHOP, I WANDERED THROUGH RIVERBEND PARK.

THERE I DITCHED THE GUN REX'S HIT MAN HAD USED ON ME.

THEN I DUCKED INTO A STALL IN THE PARK BATHROOM AND CHANGED INTO MY STARLING OUTFIT.

I SET OFF FOR THE NORWOOD MUSEUM WITH THE PAINTING TUCKED UNDER MY ARM.

NORWOOD ART MUSEUM

THE MUSEUM DIRECTOR WAS ABJECTLY GRATEFUL.

I can't thank you enough.

HE UNWOUND THE WRAPPINGS WITH PAINSTAKING CARE.

Ah, yes... safe and sound.

HE TIPPED THE CANVAS FORWARD SO I COULD SEE.

This is the painting you were looking for??

That's the one.

IT WAS STYLIZED AND SEMIABSTRACT, BUT THERE WAS NO MISTAKING IT...

IT WAS ME AT AGE TEN, UNHAPPILY WAKING UP ON A SATURDAY MORNING UNDER A PILE OF CATS.

MY MOM HAD SNAPPED IT WITH HER DISPOSABLE CAMERA, WANTING TO GET HER FAVORITE CAT, FLUFFY, AND HER OFFSPRING INTO A PICTURE.

Say "Cheese," my pretty kitties!

AS FAR AS I KNEW, THE ORIGINAL PHOTO STILL LIVED IN A BASKET OF SNAPSHOTS UNDER THE TV AT MY PARENTS' HOUSE.

How did you manage to track the painting down, by the way?

I WAS FEELING LIGHT-HEADED.

I, uh—it was just a long string of anonymous tips, really...

I'm afraid it's nothing that would enable us to get to the bottom of what happened or who took it.

Well, in our business, we're just happy to get these things back.

...aren't we, Hans?

THE CONTEMPORARY CURATOR LOOKED UNCOMFORTABLE.

Of course.

I FOLLOWED HANS BACK TO HIS OFFICE.

So this painting — is it an important work?

Well, you know, with these brand-new works, it's a bit early to tell which will stand the test of time.

Ok, but is the, uh... artist well-known?

No... I can't say he's made much of a name for himself at this point.

He's an anonymous street artist along the lines of Banksy... Certainly not a household name.

Do you have any information for the painting on file?

Sure — you can read it if you like.

PAINTING #37

Edgy & Emerging

#37 "Too Many Cats" by ARTron

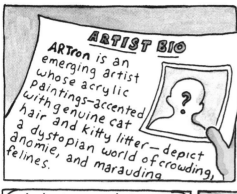

ARTIST BIO

ARTron is an emerging artist whose acrylic paintings—accented with genuine cat hair and kitty litter—depict a dystopian world of crowding, anomie, and marauding felines.

And, uh, how did you decide to include the work of this particular artist in the show?

Well, his themes...

... and the, uh, technical aspects...

...they, uh... <sigh>

To be honest? I can't remember.

It is a big show.

Yes, and a lot of these artists are relative unknowns, brand-new to the museum circuit.

But most of these pieces— I look at them and I can tell you exactly how the artist and their work came to my attention...

But this one? I look at it and I just draw a total blank.

I STUDIED THE IMAGE IN THE FILE.

And is it your feeling that this picture doesn't actually deserve to be here?

No...

The central human figure is a bit insipid...

But overall, the composition is striking, and the unconventional use of organic animal matter lends the piece gravitas.

So is this an artist you think might be going places?

Honestly? After all the attention this work is about to get from its theft and return? I can't imagine this guy's career isn't about to explode.

?

BACK IN MY CIVILIAN CLOTHES, I HEADED OVER TO MATT'S, EAGER TO HASH OUT WITH HIM THE STRANGE EVENTS OF THE DAY.

BUT MATT WAS STILL DOWNSTAIRS WORKING.

AND WITHIN MINUTES, I HAD ZONKED OUT ON THE FUTON.

BY THE TIME I WOKE UP, IT WAS MORNING.

MATT HAD COME AND GONE.

AND ALREADY I WAS LATE FOR WORK.

DAN SUMMONED ME TO HIS OFFICE AT 11:30.

Amy— my office in 1/2 hr. —D

I WAS IN A CHIPPER MOOD, LOOKING FORWARD TO CELE-BRATING THE TRIUMPH OF THE E-READER MEETING.

BUT DAN LOOKED GRIM.

Jason tells me you missed part of the meeting yesterday.

?

I was 15 minutes late. But that was because—

Amy, this was the most important day of your career here.

And it went well! They're excited to work with us.

Yes, I know. Jason told me he was able to smooth things over with them and that things are moving for-ward under his direction.

Wait—what?! That's not how things went.

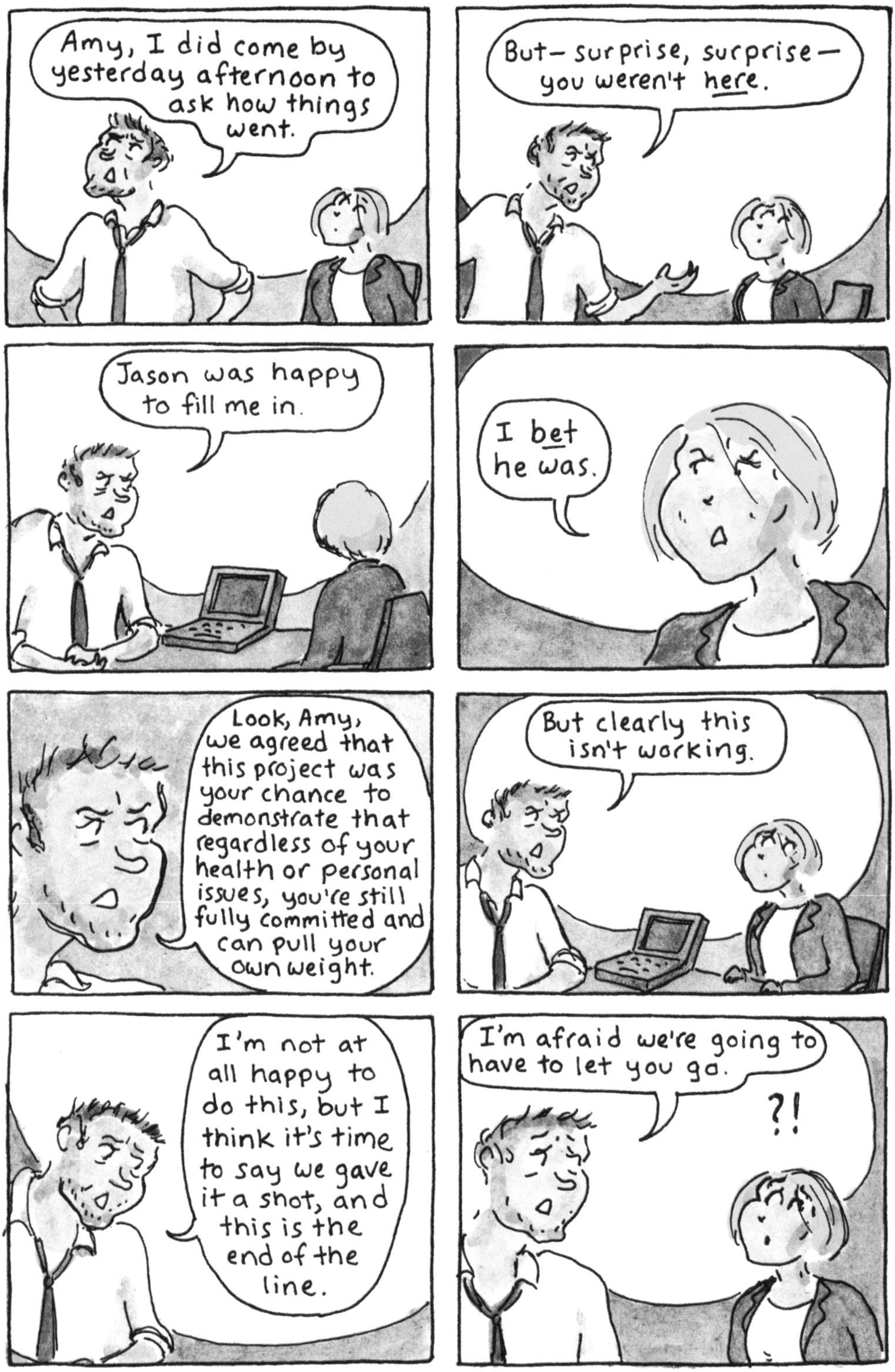
Amy, I did come by yesterday afternoon to ask how things went.
But— surprise, surprise— you weren't here.
Jason was happy to fill me in.
I bet he was.
Look, Amy, we agreed that this project was your chance to demonstrate that regardless of your health or personal issues, you're still fully committed and can pull your own weight.
But clearly this isn't working.
I'm not at all happy to do this, but I think it's time to say we gave it a shot, and this is the end of the line.
I'm afraid we're going to have to let you go.
?!

IN SHOCK, I WENT BACK TO MY OFFICE TO PACK UP MY STUFF.

Stupid, idiotic, conniving...

BY 2:30, MY THINGS WERE ALL BOXED UP.

I LEFT A NOTE ON DINA'S CHAIR...

Dina, I'm so sorry— this is not how I...

...AND TURNED IN MY KEY WITH THE OFFICE MANAGER.

Amy—?

Don't ask.

FINALLY I HEADED BACK TO MY OFFICE TO COLLECT MY STUFF.

There she is!

IT WAS THE TOP PEOPLE FROM THE SOLARIS TEAM.

We thought you were meeting with us this afternoon about next steps.

That was the original plan.

Yes—it was.

Look, there's been a little "organizational reshuffling." I'm afraid I'm not going to be working with you on the e-reader after all.

But we thought we had a —

Believe me — so did I.

But, hey — it looks like Jason is all set to get going on it with you.

Um, yes — OK. But, see — we're not really convinced that Jason is quite the right person for the project.

Without you, the whole endorsement deal with Starling and Matt McRae falls through.

And to be honest, we just don't think Jason gets the vision for the reader that you outlined.

If it's not you who's going to be our point person here, I'm afraid we're going to have to look into going with another firm.

Yeah, well. Let me know who you end up going with. Maybe I can get a job there.

What do you mean?

As it happens, I just spent the day dismantling my office and packing up, because—

...because she's moving her things to a bigger office down the hall.

And I've just turned in my keys to Sharon, so—

...so that Sharon can give you the keys to your new office.

?

Yes— apologies, all, for the misunderstanding...

Amy is out of commission for today because she needs to get herself organized in light of the promotion she's getting— and to move into her new digs.

...But once that's squared away, I know she's looking forward to a productive relationship with you, overseeing this project to its completion.

Isn't that right, Amy?

OK— SO DAN WAS A LITTLE INCONSISTENT.

...I WAS WILLING TO LIVE WITH THAT.

Um, yes—absolutely.

BY THE TIME THE DAY WAS DONE, DAN HAD REVIEWED WITH ME THE DETAILS ABOUT MY RAISE AND MY EXPANDED RESPONSIBILITIES...

...AND MY STUFF WAS ALL NICELY ARRANGED IN MY SPACIOUS NEW OFFICE.

I WAS BURSTING TO SHARE MY NEWS WITH SOMEONE.

BUT DINA WAS STILL AWAY.

AND I THOUGHT BETTER OF CALLING CLAIRE, SEEING AS I HAD A DATE WITH HER BOYFRIEND LATER THAT EVENING.

I FOUND A MESSAGE ON MY CELL PHONE.

Voicemail from: *Nikki*

NOAH WAS APPARENTLY RECOVERING FROM HIS SURGERY AND READY FOR VISITORS.

I HEADED TO THE HOSPITAL.

Noah...

Amy.

So what's the deal, little brother? Do you have a death wish or what?

No. I'm just stupid.

You are kind of an idiot. But you're definitely not stupid.

I just wish you'd told me about all the crap you were dealing with.

Yeah, well— I didn't want you to know.

So here's a question for you...

What can you tell me about a cutting-edge street artist named ARTron, whose media of choice include cat hair and kitty litter?

I don't know what you're —

Noah, I've seen the painting.

...which, I should say, looks awfully familiar, considering that's me in the middle of it.

I returned it to the museum.

What?!

No!

Yeah, yeah — I know. That was supposed to be your Get Out of Debt Free card.

Trust me. It was never going to do you any good as some kind of black-market bargaining chip.

You don't understand — I am so screwed.

Look, let me take care of Rex. But can you just please do me one favor and focus on keeping the hell away from lowlifes like him?

POOR NOAH LOOKED AS DESPONDENT AS I'D EVER SEEN HIM.

You know, the curator at the Norwood Museum says ARTron is a really talented artist.

He does?

In fact, he thinks the guy's career is poised to take off.

Really.

Yes, which means "ARTron" probably doesn't need to take security-guard jobs anymore to get his work into museum collections.

... or filch them back and pawn them off on drug-dealing creeps to try to get money for them.

... So "ARTron" might want to think about keeping up with his painting.

Maybe he will.

FOR THE FIRST TIME IN A LONG TIME, I THOUGHT JUST MAYBE NOAH WAS GOING TO BE OK.

See you later—Art Boy.

FROM THE HOSPITAL, I HEADED OVER TO MATT'S TO GET READY FOR MY DATE.

Looking Pretty for Dummies

I ALMOST SMASHED INTO MATT COMING OUT THE DOOR.

Tonight's your date, huh?

Such as it is.

Well, I should let you run.

See you later...

RUSSELL HAD PICKED A FRENCH RESTAURANT IN HONOR OF HOW WE'D MET.

Very nice.

Yes, I love this place.

IT WAS A LOVELY EVENING.

WE TALKED ABOUT OUR WORK.

...so then at the last minute, the judge did give us an extension.

AND WE REMINISCED ABOUT SCHOOL.

I always say—nothing beats the way the sun used to come right up over alumni field.

HE TOOK MY HAND.

TO MY RELIEF, IT STAYED BENIGNLY VOLTAGE-FREE.

AFTER ALL THESE YEARS, MAYBE THIS WAS FINALLY GOING TO WORK.

HE ORDERED CHAMPAGNE WITH OUR DESSERT.

A toast!

To you... finally succumbing to my charms!

Yes, to...

...to...

Are you ok?

Is it Claire?

Yes...

No...

Actually, I'm sorry—

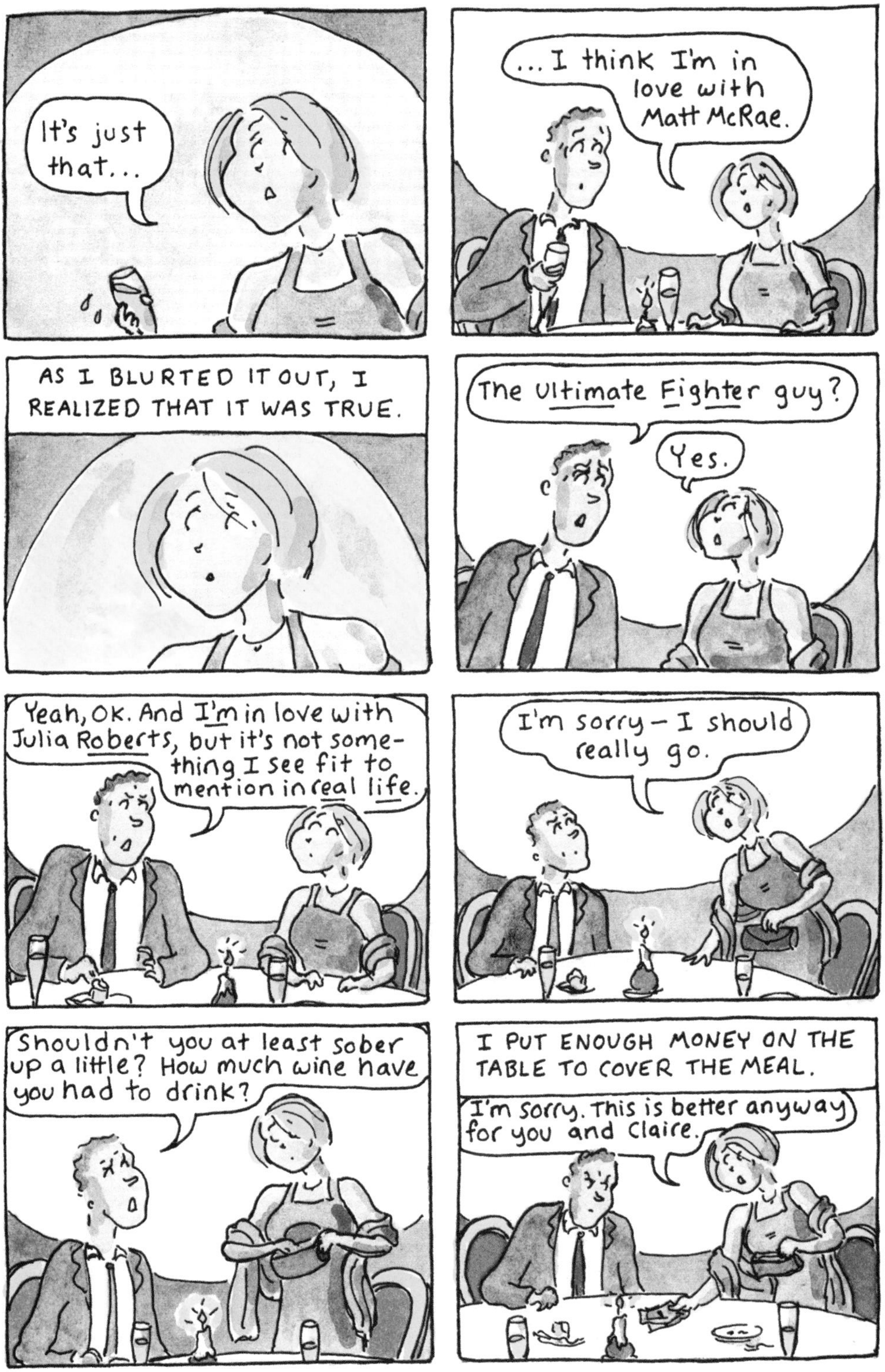
It's just that...
...I think I'm in love with Matt McRae.
AS I BLURTED IT OUT, I REALIZED THAT IT WAS TRUE.
The Ultimate Fighter guy?
Yes.
Yeah, OK. And I'm in love with Julia Roberts, but it's not something I see fit to mention in real life.
I'm sorry – I should really go.
Shouldn't you at least sober up a little? How much wine have you had to drink?
I PUT ENOUGH MONEY ON THE TABLE TO COVER THE MEAL.
I'm sorry. This is better anyway for you and Claire.

I HURRIED BACK TO MATT'S APARTMENT WITH A SENSE OF RESOLVE.

IN MY HEAD, I TRIED TO WORK OUT WHAT I WAS GOING TO SAY.

Matt, can we talk for a minute?

Matt, I have a confession...

AT THE DOOR TO HIS APARTMENT, I TOOK A DEEP BREATH.

Matt, I...

Oh!...I'm sorry!

Hey.

I'm Natasha.

I'm sorry—I came back early.

SHE BUSTLED OUT IN A CLOUD OF PERFUME.

I TRIED TO HIDE MY DISMAY.

BUT ANNOYINGLY, MATT KEPT HOVERING.

We used to date. She's a UFC ring girl.

NO WONDER SHE LOOKED LIKE BARBIE.

She's very pretty.

I wanted her advice about yo—

It's your own apartment. You don't have to explain.

Amy, I—

Excuse me—I really need to get some sleep.

OF COURSE, MY BUZZER WENT OFF IN THE MIDDLE OF THE NIGHT.

ALERT: Hold up, Aram's QuikMart, Rt. 30

You want company?

No — I got it.

BUT BEATING PEOPLE UP ALONE IN THE MIDDLE OF THE NIGHT WAS EVEN MORE DEPRESSING THAN USUAL.

THE KID HOLDING UP THE CONVENIENCE STORE WAS CLEARLY JUST SOME DESPERATE DRUGGIE.

WE CARD

IGNORING PROTOCOL AS USUAL, I DRAGGED HIM PAST THE POLICE STATION.

POLICE

Trust me — that's where you're going next time.

I BROUGHT HIM INSTEAD TO THE REHAB FACILITY ON 16TH STREET.

NEW DAY

I WISHED HIM THE BEST AS I HANDED HIM OFF.

Take care of yourself.

Screw off.

IT SEEMED LIKE REASONABLE ADVICE.

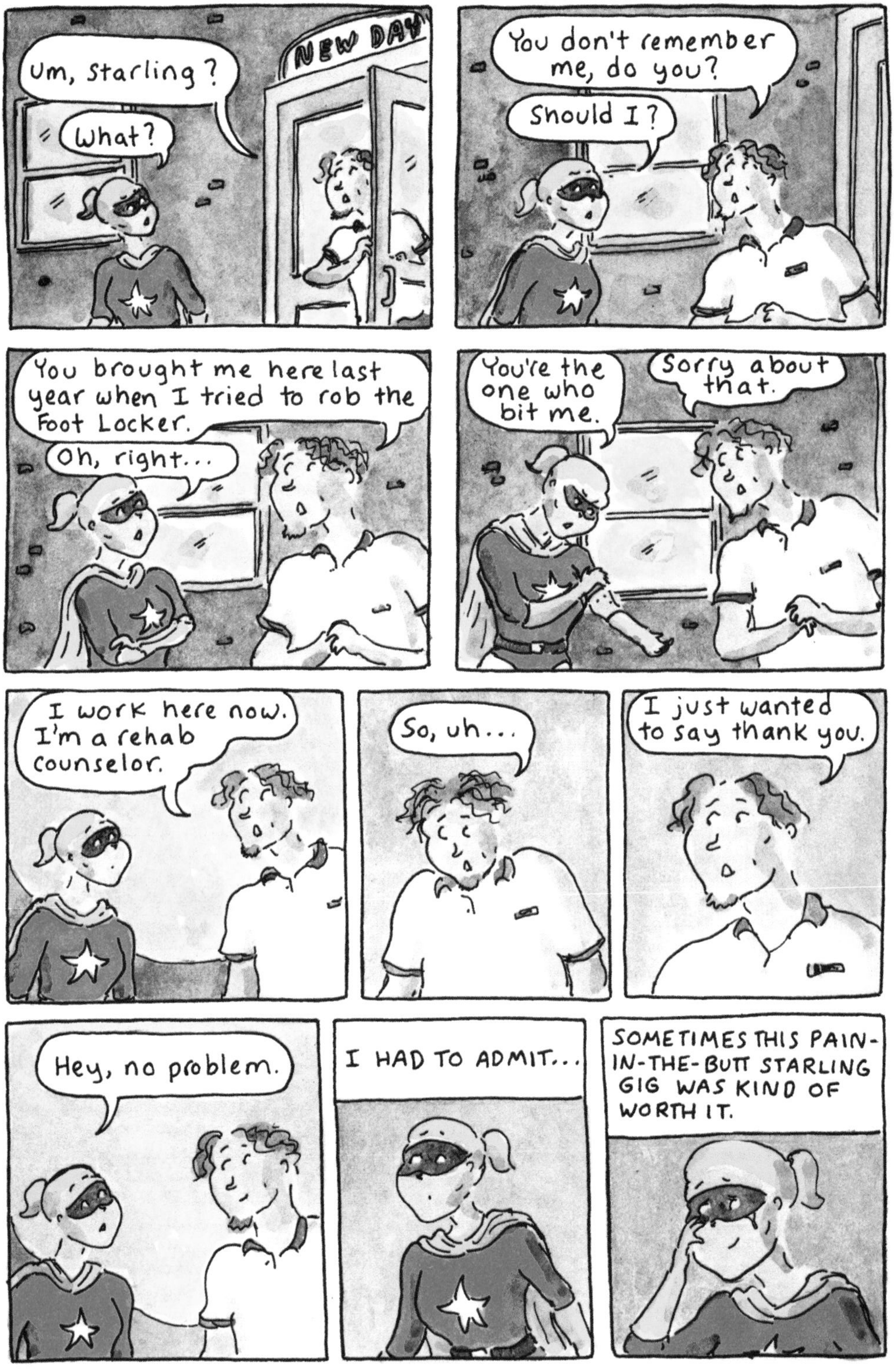
NEW DAY
Um, Starling?
What?
You don't remember me, do you?
Should I?
You brought me here last year when I tried to rob the Foot Locker.
Oh, right...
You're the one who bit me.
Sorry about that.
I work here now. I'm a rehab counselor.
So, uh...
I just wanted to say thank you.
Hey, no problem.
I HAD TO ADMIT...
SOMETIMES THIS PAIN-IN-THE-BUTT STARLING GIG WAS KIND OF WORTH IT.

AT LUNCHTIME THE NEXT DAY, I WENT TO THE BANK.

THE SOLARIS PEOPLE HAD GIVEN ME A BIG CHUNK OF CHANGE TO PASS ON TO STARLING AS AN ADVANCE FOR HER PRODUCT ENDORSEMENT.

SOLARIS Co.
STARLING
(C/O A. Sturgess)

I CASHED THE CHECK.

THEN I PUT ON MY STARLING GEAR AND WENT LOOKING FOR REX DANIELS.

I understand that a kid named Noah owes you 15 grand.

I have payment here in full.

...which I'll hand over if you can promise you'll leave Noah alone.

You are aware, are you not, that your friend destroyed something very important to me?

You're a savvy businessman. I don't doubt you can reconstruct your operations manual, no problem.

That may be, but I'm afraid I didn't get to where I am by just letting these kinds of things go.

OH, LORD—NOT THIS AGAIN...

Look, Rex— You are aware, are you not, that one of your minions already blasted me in the chest with an assault rifle this week?

...And I think you'll notice that I'm still here, but your friend seems to be out of commission.

...I don't suppose you're hoping to find out for yourself exactly what became of him?

I CONCENTRATED HARD AND WILLED MY HANDS TO SHOOT OFF A FEW SPARKS.

HE SET THE GUN DOWN.

THANK GOD FOR THE POWER OF A GOOD BLUFF.

So we have an agreement, then.

If I hear about anything happening to Noah, I know where to find you.

CLAIRE CAME BY IN THE AFTERNOON.

Wow, look at you in your fancy new office! Congratulations!

You, too— the Solaris people love your work.

WE SPENT MORE THAN AN HOUR WORKING ON A GAME PLAN AND A SCHEDULE.

FINALLY, MY ATTENTION SPAN HAVING REACHED ITS LIMIT, I SAT BACK.

You seem better than last time I saw you.

Yeah— I kind of am.

Russell actually came raging drunk to my apartment last night, whining about having made a terrible mistake and wanting me back.

That's great— so are you guys good now?

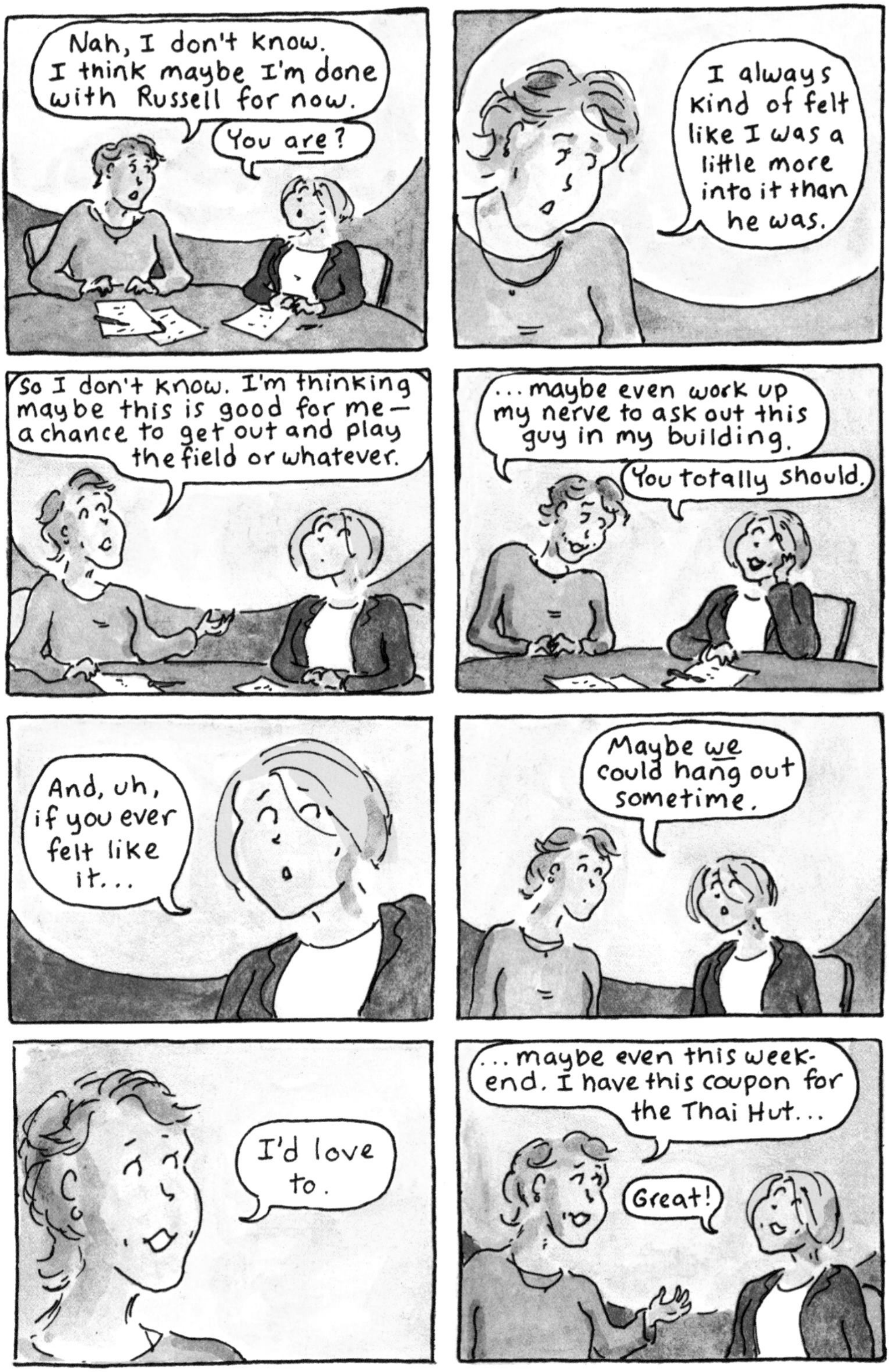
Nah, I don't know. I think maybe I'm done with Russell for now.
You are?
I always kind of felt like I was a little more into it than he was.
So I don't know. I'm thinking maybe this is good for me— a chance to get out and play the field or whatever.
...maybe even work up my nerve to ask out this guy in my building.
You totally should.
And, uh, if you ever felt like it...
Maybe we could hang out sometime.
I'd love to.
...maybe even this week-end. I have this coupon for the Thai Hut...
Great!

NOW THAT I'D CALLED OFF REX DANIELS'S GUYS, I FIGURED THERE WASN'T REALLY ANY GOOD REASON FOR ME TO KEEP HIDING OUT AT MATT'S.

I SNUCK UP TO THE APARTMENT THAT EVENING WHILE HE WAS AT WORK AND COLLECTED MY STUFF.

BACK HOME, MY OWN APARTMENT FELT DEPRESSINGLY EMPTY.

I HADN'T BEEN HOME SINCE BEFORE DINA'S WEDDING.

EVEN THE LAST OF NOAH'S STUFF HAD BEEN COLLECTED BY NIKKI.

EVENTUALLY I PUT THE TV ON FOR COMPANY AND DOZED OFF ON THE COUCH.

WHEN THE 11:00 P.M. NEWS CAME ON, I PERKED UP.

IT SEEMED THEY WERE TALKING ABOUT THE NORWOOD MUSEUM.

Since its announcement yesterday about the recovery of the painting, the museum has said that interest in the work, and in ARTron, its anonymous creator, has been overwhelming.

Through his agent, Nikki Bello, the artist has indicated a willingness to put the work up for auction with Sotheby's following the show.

Already, preliminary bids are said to be coming in close to the $1 million mark.

GEEZ— GO, NOAH!

I DECIDED I WAS DEFINITELY GOING TO MAKE HIM PAY ME BACK THAT $15,000 AFTER ALL.

A HALF HOUR LATER, I WAS AWAKENED AGAIN.

Knock
Knock
Knock

?

Crud.

Knock knock!

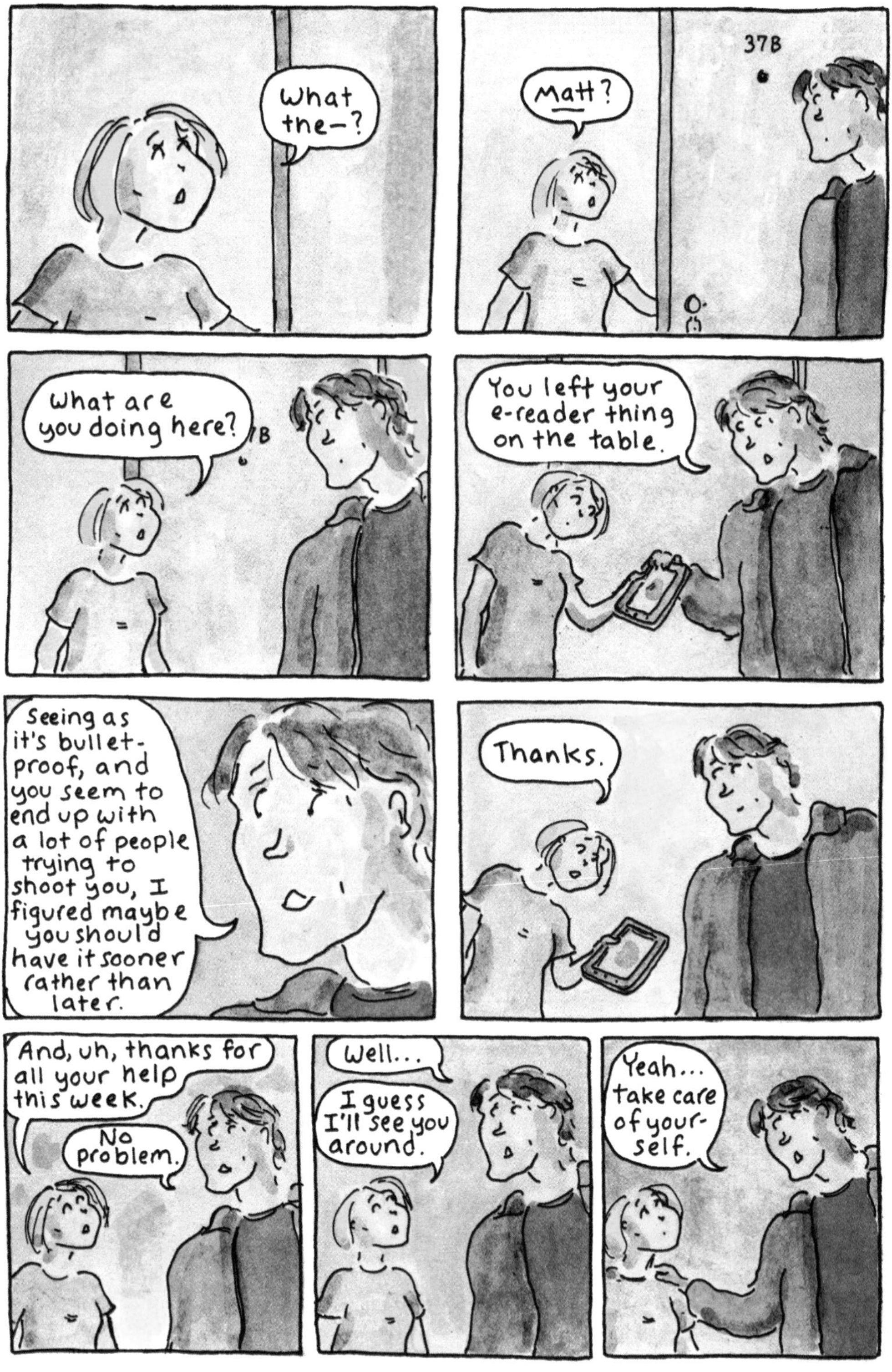
What the—?
37B
Matt?
What are you doing here?
You left your e-reader thing on the table.
Seeing as it's bullet-proof, and you seem to end up with a lot of people trying to shoot you, I figured maybe you should have it sooner rather than later.
Thanks.
And, uh, thanks for all your help this week.
No problem.
Well...
I guess I'll see you around.
Yeah... take care of your-self.

WITH A SINKING FEELING, I WATCHED HIM HEAD BACK OUT INTO THE NIGHT.

HE WASN'T EVEN TO THE STAIRS WHEN THE INTERCOM BUZZED.

Hello?

Aymeeee

OH, LORD...

Russell?

HE WAS CLEARLY DRUNK.

Can I pleeeze come up? I just need to talk to yooo.

<sigh> I'm sorry, Russell. I think you should go home and drink a bunch of water.

What do you care? You don't love me.

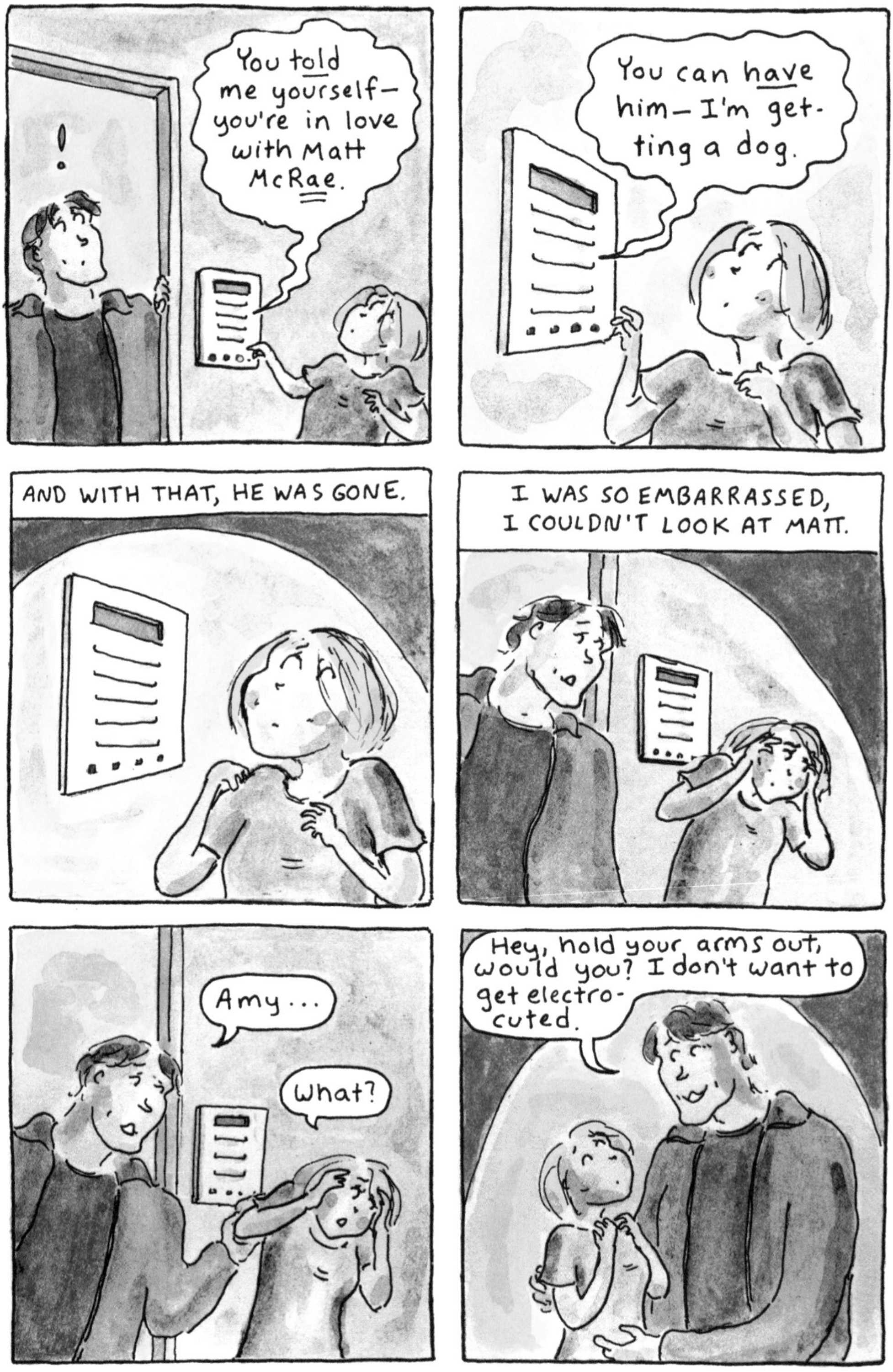

You told me yourself—you're in love with Matt McRae.
You can have him— I'm getting a dog.
AND WITH THAT, HE WAS GONE.
I WAS SO EMBARRASSED, I COULDN'T LOOK AT MATT.
Amy...
What?
Hey, hold your arms out, would you? I don't want to get electrocuted.

AT 4:30 A.M. MY BUZZER WENT OFF.

I have to go.

Can I come with you?

You may.

OK, SO MAYBE MY LITTLE PROCRASTINATION PROBLEM WASN'T ABOUT TO GET ANY BETTER.

BUT AS FOR THE REST?...

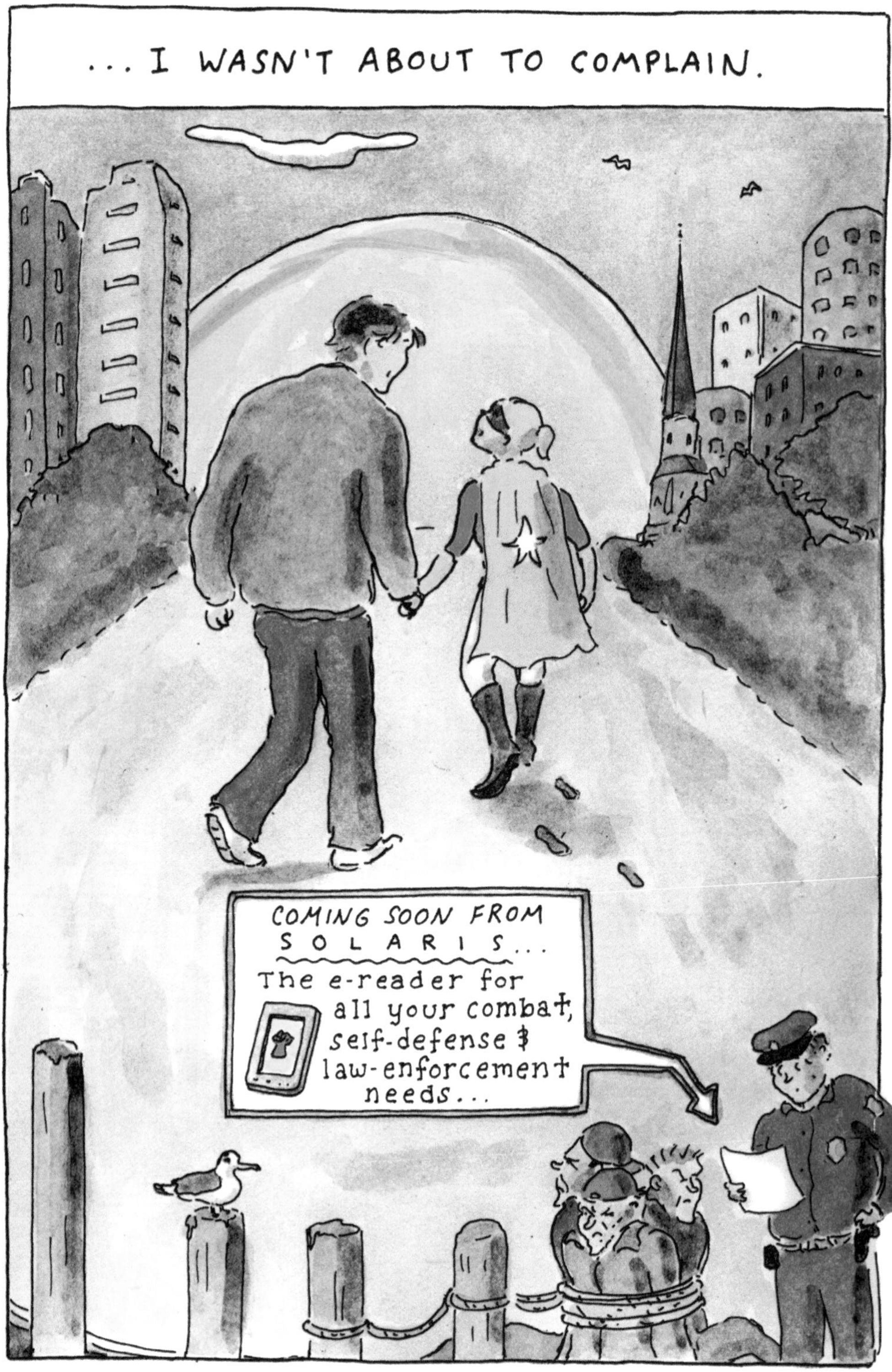

... I WASN'T ABOUT TO COMPLAIN.
COMING SOON FROM SOLARIS...
The e-reader for all your combat, self-defense & law-enforcement needs...

Sage Stossel is a contributing editor at *The Atlantic*, drawing the cartoon feature *Sage, Ink*, and is the author of the children's books *On the Loose in Boston* and *On the Loose in Washington, D.C.* She is also a regular contributor to *The Boston Globe* and *Provincetown Banner*, for which she received an award in 2009 from the New England Newspaper & Press Association. Her cartoons have been featured by *The New York Times* Week in Review, CNN Headline News, CartoonArts International / *The New York Times Syndicate*, and *Best Editorial Cartoons of the Year* (2005, 2006, 2009, and 2010 editions).

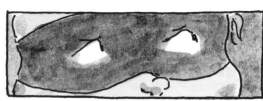